A LIFE ALTERING DISCOVERY

not everyone has a soul

SHAHAN SHAMMAS

WORTHWHILE PUBLICATIONS

Copyright © 2025 SHAHAN SHAMMAS

All rights reserved

Copyright © 2025 by Shahan Shammas. All rights reserved. No part of this book may be reproduced or transmitted in any form or by any means, electronic or mechanical, including photocopying, recording, or by an information storage and retrieval system–except by a reviewer who may quote brief passages in a review to be printed in a book, magazine or newspaper–without permission in writing from the publisher. For information, please contact Worthwhile Publications or the author at shahanshammas@gmail.com

Although the author and publisher have made every effort to ensure the accuracy and completeness of information contained in this book, we assume no responsibility for errors, inaccuracies, omissions, or any inconsistencies herein. Any slights on people, places, or organizations are unintentional.

ISBN-13: 9780966202854

Printed in the United States of America

To my wife, Barbara, and my daughters Olivia and Emily and their husbands Ben and Antony. To my grandchildren Dylan and Chloe. To the brave souls everywhere unafraid to question their beliefs, open their eyes to see, clear their ears to hear and examine their hearts to discern the truth.

CONTENTS

Title Page	
Copyright	
Dedication	
Introduction	1
Part I	4
Does Everyone Have a Soul?	5
Part II	24
Out-of-Body Experience (OBE)	25
Near-Death Experience (NDE)	27
Soul Visitations	29
Answers to Prayers	33
Dreams	35
Why Attraction?	37
Hypnotherapy	40
Biology	42
Self-Sacrifice	44
The Changeless	46
A Test	48
Synchronicity	50

Part III	52
The Sublime	53
Part IV	59
Love	60
Beauty	62
Joy	64
Secondary Attributes	67
Inspiration	68
Creativity, Imagination, Visualization	70
Sympathy, Empathy and Compassion	72
Service	75
Forgiveness	77
Character and Personality	79
Part V	81
Dimensions and Reality	82
The Composition of Soul	84
The Purpose of Life	89
A Simple Way to Experience Soul	91
Does the Soul Need to be Saved?	93
Part VI	102
An Interesting Thought	103
4 Questions	106
Final Thoughts	109
How One Book Altered the Course of My Life	114
Acknowledgement	129
About The Author	131

… Books By This Author

INTRODUCTION

There are times in our lives when we are shocked, disturbed and thrown into a tail spin. Fortunately, this rarely happens, but when it does, we never forget the incident and its aftermath which could be physical, mental, and emotional.

The first blow to my otherwise routine existence was when my mother passed away at the age of 36, leaving behind 6 children ranging in age from 3 to 15. I was 13 then. My life was never the same after that.

My second blow came as a mental and emotional shock. It was when I learned that we are just as the beasts are with no advantage over them.

> *I said in my heart with regard to the children of man that God is testing them that they may see that they themselves are but beasts. Eccl 3:18*

The third blow came when I learned that not everyone has a soul. The first time I heard this was from someone I regarded highly. As soon as I heard it, it threw me into a state of nonplus as if I was struck by lightning. It stirred me to question who might be the ones with a soul and who are the ones without a soul.

I never forgot this incident. Yet, I pushed it to the back of my mind until I was reminded of it once more in a book by

Dolores Cannon.

Dolores Cannon was a regressive hypnotherapist and a psychic researcher who recorded "lost" knowledge. She has written many books and I have purchased and read most of them. In one of her books, an individual under hypnotic regression mentioned that not everyone has a soul. My intrigue was piqued and my interest was rekindled.

It was Shakespeare who wrote that life was a stage and we are actors on this stage. In my book **<u>Know Yourself, Love Yourself, Express Yourself,</u>** *an inspiring guide to intentional living*, I have a chapter titled: ***We Are in a Theater***. I wrote that we live in the theater of life. We enter this theater at birth and we exit it at death. In the theater of life, we are either actors, directors, the ones helping behind the scenes, or the audience.

Actors require an audience, support personnel and directors. Actors are few, directors and the support personnel are the required number while the audience is a multitude. Actors, directors and support personnel live to make a difference. The audience is there looking to be entertained and amused. What I did not mention in that chapter is that actors, directors and support personnel must have souls while the majority of the audience, who are mere props making it possible for the actors to act out their roles, do not have souls.

Each actor on stage, whether in a theater or the larger arena of life, has a purpose for being there, a mission that they must fulfill, hopefully with distinction. Those who labor behind the scenes, do important work yet they remain anonymous. While not all actors are equally "talented", the audience is all the same in that they are observers. They can decide to remain quiet, respond by cheering the actors on or they can boo the performance. That is the extent of their involvement.

Those on the stage of life who accept a mission for their lives and strive to achieve it have well-developed souls.

Those working behind the scenes are actively building up their souls. Those who passively squander their time and resources by being a "prop" throughout their lives, even if they have the remnants of a soul now, will lose it once they die.

* * * * *

We have been endowed with an initial spark, a seed in the form of a soul. This is the one "talent" we are all born with. According to the teachings of Christ through the parables, we are expected to at least double this one talent each lifetime. (See my book **The Secret Teachings of Christ based on the parables**).

The parable of the talents makes it clear that if we bury our talent in the soil, or do not invest it by nurturing it and allowing it to grow and multiply, then even the one talent that we start life with (our initial soul), will be taken away from us and we will be left without any soul. In other words, use it or lose it. Whether or not we end up having a soul or not is entirely up to us. We have our entire life to decide to be an actor and act, support personnel and contribute, or be entertained as a member of the audience. Once we die, it is judgment time. If we have nurtured our soul by adding to it, then we end up with an epi-soul, a growing and maturing soul. Otherwise, we will not have a soul and once we die, that is our end, dust to dust, earth to earth. We will no longer exist. (The concept of epi-soul is explained in my book, **Mystery Solved! human immortality revealed**.

The good news is that we have a choice. Our fate is in our hands based on how we decide to live our lives. My books make it amply clear what the purpose of life is. If we use a small portion of our allocated time and resources to cultivate and nurture our souls, then we will not only ensure that we have a soul but also guarantee our immortality.

PART I

DOES EVERYONE HAVE A SOUL?

DOES EVERYONE HAVE A SOUL?

The beautiful souls of the world have an art of saintly alchemy, by which bitterness is converted into kindness, the gall of human experience into gentleness, ingratitude into benefits, insults into pardon. — Henri Frederic Amiel

Undeniably, the most important question we need an answer for is, "Do we have a soul and if we do, is it immortal?"

The answer to the question of whether or not the soul is real or a fanciful creation to appease and comfort people is neither obvious nor easy to prove. Many religions proclaim the existence of the soul, yet none of them provide any proof of its existence.

We are expected to base our acceptance of the reality of the soul on mere belief and faith. But this question is too important to relegate it to anything other than solid proof based on experiential knowledge.

If we have a soul and it is immortal, then we can relax and enjoy our lives. We do not have to fear death, because it is then a mere passage from a physical life into an astral and spiritual life. Knowing that we have an immortal soul, we can be assured that we will continue to exist once our bodies die, disintegrate and return back to their earthly elements.

If, on the other hand, we do not have a soul, then we have to make the most out of this life because it is the only one we have and once we die, we no longer exist—we are gone forever, blotted out of existence.

There is a third option. What if we begin life with a soul, like a seed dropped into the soil? If the seed falls on fertile soil, establishes a root system and grows, then we end up with a soul. Otherwise, we do not.

What if it is up to us whether we end up with a soul or not?

I am not a believer. I cannot and will not base my life on a belief that no one has been able to prove one way or the other. I must know beyond any doubt. So, my quest for an answer is on.

My desire to know whether or not we have a soul began very early in my life. You could even say that it was my fate to tackle this question.

* * * * *

Many of us have a few indelible memories from childhood, memories that we can never forget. Why do we remember certain things but not others? Why do some events hit us in the gut and change us forever? I have several of these memories. One in particular is when I was about 9 years old when my Uncle Jacob handed me the Bible and asked me to read a passage for him. Here is that passage:

> *I said in my heart with regard to the children of man that God is testing them that they may see that they themselves are but beasts. For what happens to the children of man and what happens to the beasts is the same; as one dies, so dies the other. They all have the same breath, and man has no advantage over the beasts, for all is vanity. All go to one place. All are from the dust, and to dust all return. Who knows whether the spirit of man goes upward and the spirit of the beast goes down into the earth? So I saw that there is nothing better than that a man should rejoice in his work, for that is his lot. Who can bring him to see what will be after him?* Eccl. 3:18-22

As soon as I finished reading this passage, something in me revolted. I do not know whether it was my ego or the shock to my rock-solid belief that this cannot be true since everyone knows that we are different from beasts – we can talk! But then again, this passage is in the Bible! It must be true. But how can it be? Humans are not beasts, at least not to my way of thinking back then.

This incident left such an indelible mark on my consciousness that I never forgot it. I refer to it in several of my books, especially my first book, **_A Passion for Living_**, **_a path to meaning and joy_**.

This passage haunted me. I had to know. I had to find out.

* * * * *

As I mentioned at the beginning, my mother passed away

when I was 13 years old. She died as a result of abuse by my father. She was 36 years old. She left behind 6 children ranging in age from 3 to 15 years old.

My dad was a talented young man. He was skilled, but could not hold onto a job because of his temper. He worked as a day laborer in a bakery whenever he could, but often, because of his temper and frustration with his situation, he would start a fight, quit or be fired.

My father never earned enough money to take care of his family – a wife and 6 young children. So, my mother would often work at a factory or clean people's homes for some extra cash or donations of food or clothing. At times, she would send me to clean a house and/or collect donations. I did not mind the work, yet I resented having to accept donations. It was demeaning.

*****

My dad was not only abusive to my mother to the extent that he caused her death by a blunt strike on her head, he also took out his frustrations on me. I endured countless brutal physical beatings. For a long time, I resented my dad. I was young and did not know any better. I did not realize how one's circumstances can bring out the worst in a human being. Living in extreme poverty, not being able to feed and clothe his family or even pay rent, placed such an enormous burden on my dad. He was talented and capable, yet lacked the opportunity to contribute. My dad is a good example of how one's circumstances shape one's character and personality.

*****

Immediately after my mother's death, our lives were

changed forever. My father could not take care of us before and it was even more difficult now that my mother was no longer around to help out. So, after a fight with my older brother, he asked my brother to leave and never come back home again. My brother, not only left home permanently; he left Syria and went to Lebanon. My father then arranged to place my two youngest brothers in an orphanage, gave up my sister for adoption and arranged with our church for me to go to Lebanon and join a monastery to study for the clergy.

* * * * *

Looking back on my life, I never realized the significance of these events while they were taking place. How we interpret an event while it is happening is very different from our interpretation of that same event years later.

When my mother passed away, it was the worst thing that could have happened to our family. She was the glue that held our family together. Yet, because she passed away, we had an opportunity to disperse and seek out new lives.

It was not easy for us. We struggled. We experienced dejection, loneliness, even hunger and the feeling of being lost with no one who cared. I now realize the full significance of what we went through. It built our characters and shaped our personalities. Having experienced lack of family life, we learned to value family relationships. Having known hunger, we appreciated sufficiency. Having experienced dejection, we developed empathy. Not knowing love, we can now experience it with our loved ones. It is not only experiences that shape our lives, but also our interpretations of what these experiences mean and what we make of them. Additionally, unforeseen events, especially synchronicities, have a major role in shaping us and determining our destiny.

I often ask myself why I was sent to the monastery. Was it for mere convenience? Or, is there more to it? In my later years, I came to believe that there is much more to our lives than what is apparent. There are unseen forces that we are unaware of. These forces make themselves evident through the synchronicities we encounter. I now fully appreciate all that I have experienced. Every event and each experience was like a piece of a gigantic puzzle. These pieces were scattered all over space and time. Once I put these pieces into their proper place, a clear and unambiguous picture began to emerge of the purpose and mission of my life. We are each being trained and prepared through our experiences to carry out the mission for which we were born.

The question each of us should be asking is, "Now that I have these experiences, what is the best use I can put them to?" The answer is clear. We must make the most of our opportunities by pursuing our passion, contributing to the welfare of others and by investing a portion of our time and resources to cultivate our minds and enrich our souls. We must endeavor to improve the quality of life for everyone starting with our family. We must always start where we are and work with what we currently have. By engaging in continuous education and by honing our skills, our contributions to society continuously improve. In my case, I embraced not only continuous education and self-improvement, but also undertook teaching, writing and speaking. I accepted my mission in life to be a light that dispels darkness, especially ignorance, bigotry and a false sense of self-importance at the expense of others. My aim is to make a difference. Any contribution I make is far better than no contribution at all.

* * * * *

Monastery life was serene, peaceful and routine. I was content and happy. The head monk, Father Isaac Saka, favored me and often asked me to help him with his manuscript writings. We studied Aramaic, scriptures, the sciences and theology. We had a routine that was comforting. Early morning prayers, breakfast, classes, lunch, afternoon studies, evening prayers, dinner and personal study time until bedtime, Monday through Friday. Saturdays, we had more free time including time to go on long walks on the mountain and in the fields. On Sundays we went to church in the city to participate in mass.

Everyone participated in mass, except for me. I had everything going for me, being the head monk's favorite student, except for my voice. In the Syriac Orthodox Church that I belonged to, mass is mostly chanted with the participation of the deacons and the clergy. I could not carry a tune and no one wanted to hear me chant. So, after a while no one bothered to ask me to participate.

Was my lack of a good voice a curse or a blessing?

In the short term and in the narrow view, my inability to chant was a curse especially since I belonged to the clergy and I was expected to chant. In the long term and in the broader view, however, this was a blessing in disguise. It helped me decide if I belonged in the monastery.

I stayed at the monastery for two years during which time I avoided chanting. I continued my religious and academic studies. I also had a few unforgettable experiences.

The first of these unforgettable experiences was my mother's visit to me. I describe this incident in detail in my first book, ***A Passion for Living, a path to meaning and joy***. My mother visited and comforted me after she had been dead for some time.

The second incident was a lucid dream in which I experienced events that I came to verify later on. This was my first lucid dream and I never forgot it.

The third incident was the erosion of my faith in the god of the Old Testament. This happened during several incidents. The first was during a theology class where my teacher was explaining the events of a story that took place. In answer to Hezekiah's prayer, the Lord sent his angel to strike down and murder 185,000 Assyrian soldiers. Here is the verse:

> And that night the angel of the LORD went out and struck down 185,000 in the camp of the Assyrians. And when people arose early in the morning, behold, these were all dead bodies. 2Kgs 19:35

The second incident happened while I was studying the Bible on my own. I was reading the story of the Exodus when I came across the following verses:

> But I will harden Pharaoh's heart, and though I multiply my signs and wonders in the land of Egypt, Pharaoh will not listen to you. Then I will lay my hand on Egypt and bring my hosts, my people the children of Israel, out of the land of Egypt by great acts of judgment. The Egyptians shall know that I am the LORD, when I stretch out my hand against Egypt and bring out the people of Israel from among them." Exod 7:3-5

> *But the LORD hardened the heart of Pharaoh, and he did not listen to them, as the LORD had spoken to Moses. Exod 9:12*

I had to read these verses over and over. I was stunned. I could not believe what I was reading. Why would the Lord intentionally harden the Pharoh's heart so he could inflict horrendous plagues and afflictions on the Egyptians while sparing the Israelites?

And when I read about the killing of all the first born of the Egyptians, that tipped the scale. I could no longer remain silent. I openly revolted.

> *Moses and Aaron did all these wonders before Pharaoh, and the LORD hardened Pharaoh's heart, and he did not let the people of Israel go out of his land. Exod 11:10*
>
> *At midnight the LORD struck down all the firstborn in the land of Egypt, from the firstborn of Pharaoh who sat on his throne to the firstborn of the captive who was in the dungeon, and all the firstborn of the livestock. And Pharaoh rose up in the night, he and all his servants and all the Egyptians. And there was a great cry in Egypt, for there was not a house where someone was not dead. Exod 12:29-30*

My heart was torn apart. What if I had lost my first born child? Would I believe and worship such a bloodthirsty murderer who intentionally hardens hearts so he could inflict pain and suffering on innocent people when the whole drama could be avoided if he did the opposite? From that day on, I no longer believed that the god of the Old Testament can truly be a God. I was fearless in my rejection of this so-called deity. I no longer believed the Bible to be either the word of God or even inspired writing. I was transformed. I was born anew—fearless, questioning my beliefs and examining what was handed down as my heritage.

I soon realized that even those we consider to be heroes in the Bible are not so. Consider the case of Abraham. Imagine you are a father with only one child. Imagine that you hear a voice, have a dream or an angel asks you to sacrifice your son to demonstrate your obedience and absolute faith. Would you do it? I would not, I would look that source in the eyes and quoting Christ would say: *Get thee behind me, Satan!*

> But he turned, and said unto Peter, Get thee behind me, Satan: thou art an offence unto me: for thou savourest not the things that be of God, but those that be of men. Matt 16:23 (KJV)

What kind of people are we if we are willing to sacrifice our children to demonstrate faith or obedience? What kind of a god are we worshipping if he demands it?

I could no longer stay in the monastery. I even began to question whether any God existed at all. For a while, I became an atheist.

* * * * *

After 2 years in the monastery, I left at the end of February 1964. I started high school in Sidon, Lebanon in March 1964 after Spring Break. In June 1967, I graduated from high school and through an incredible series of synchronicities, I was able to attend the American University of Beirut.

* * * * *

After leaving Aleppo, Syria for Lebanon, I left all family, relatives, and friends behind. I was mostly on my own. The only person I knew was Aunt Faith. She was an American missionary for whom my mother had worked as a cleaning lady while Aunt Faith lived in Aleppo before she moved to Lebanon. (She is not related to us. We call her Aunt Faith out of respect).

Looking back on my life, I can clearly see that synchronicities played a critical role in shaping me. Not only was it synchronicity that enabled me to attend college, I also managed to stay there until I was ready to leave for the United States.

I came to Lebanon to study religion and join the clergy. The Syrian government allows young people to do that and exempts them from conscription. Now that I was no longer in the monastery, I had no legal status to be in Lebanon. I could not return to Syria, for if I did, I would be conscripted.

Once more, through an incredible series of synchronistic events, I was granted a permanent visa to immigrate to the United States. Having no passport, the International Red Cross issued a paper stating that I was without a country. With that paper and the visa, I left for the United States.

* * * * *

I landed in Boston, Massachusetts on February 14, 1972. After a brief stay in Massachusetts, I joined the US Army to be a food inspector. Through some more incredible synchronicities, instead of going to Ft. Sam Houston in

Texas to be a food inspector, I ended up at Fort Meade, Maryland as a medical technician.

After completing my 3-year service at Fort Meade, I rented an apartment and lived in Glen Burnie, MD. It was there that I had my second out-of-body (OBE) experience. (My first out-of-body experience is described in my first book, <u>**A Passion for Living**</u>, *a path to meaning and joy*).

* * * * *

To find oneself out of the body once is jarring enough, but to have an OBE 2 or more times led me to question my assumptions regarding the nature of reality.

Through my various OBE experiences, I learned that when I am not in my physical body, the body has no volition of its own. It cannot move, speak, hear or understand. It is me as the I AM who is living in the physical body who does all these things. Out of my physical body, I can see, hear and move about freely. Unfortunately, no physical person can see or hear me.

Through my near-death-experience (NDE), I discovered that we have two types of "software" —an "operating system" and "specialized software". The "operating system" is the same for everyone. This is what we share with the beasts. It has evolved over the millennia to what it is now. With it, we can perform all of our bodily functions. We can talk, see, hear, taste, smell, feel and function on instinct.

Our "specialized software" is due to our soul. With it we have advanced memory and we can visualize and project into the past and the future. We can imagine, meditate, pray and be creative. We can be inspired. It is our soul that gives us consciousness, conscience and freedom of choice.

(For more detail about these subjects, please refer to my books listed at the back of the book).

There is no alternative for actual personal experience to gain knowledge, wisdom and understanding. I cannot convey what I felt or experienced while out of my physical body or when I had my near-death-experience. While we can share our knowledge, we cannot impart our experiences to anyone else. Words convey information, not experience. Words are like a map of a place. We cannot experience a place by looking at its map. Even though I can describe what I experienced, I cannot impart the emotional impact these experiences had on me. Knowing only results from firsthand experience.

* * * * *

How can we discover the truth about the nature of our reality? How can we know for certain whether or not we have a soul? How can we know for sure whether or not the soul is immortal? Should we accept that we have a soul because this is what we were told? What if it is not true? We need to find out for ourselves.

We are told many "truths" by systems of thought, parents and peers. We are told that we have souls because it is written in certain books, or taught by prophets, seers, or inspired people. Statements in books and the words of others are just information until we have an experience that validates that information. Then it becomes our reality. Ultimately, the only proof that counts is that which we can demonstrate ourselves. We must be convinced because of **our** experiences. It is easy to believe. It is far more difficult to know for sure. It takes effort, intention and persistence to arrive at satisfying answers.

I began to study the literature. I read what the philosophers said about the soul. I looked for answers in the various religions. I did not find proof anywhere. I embraced continuous education earnestly and persistently as a path to learning and discovering. I sought, asked and knocked. When my questioning became overwhelming, I had my answer. I experienced a near-death event that upended my life to the core. (Described in my first book: **_A Passion for Living_**, *a path to meaning and joy*).

* * * * *

I seem to be on an accelerated path. When I was in basic training at Fort Dix in New Jersey in July of 1972, I was in the accelerated platoon. My entire life seems to be on a direct path to learn, to contribute and to actualize my potential.

While in the Army at Fort Meade, MD, I discovered the writings of Wilhelm Reich. I purchased and read all of his writings. He did extensive research on the life-force, which he called the Orgone Energy.

Next, I discovered and read the writings of Jane Roberts, who channeled the Seth material. I purchased and studied all of her books. I wondered where does this incredible, insightful and enlightening material come from? Who is Seth, a discarnate personality? How can a "spirit" being dictate through a physical human being?

Next, I discovered and joined the Rosicrucian Order, AMORC. I remained an active member for over 30 years. I was their Regional Instructor for the Middle Atlantic Region for many years conducting seminars, workshops and speaking at conclaves. I discovered that the best way to learn was to teach. If I could teach a subject, then I must know it, else I could not teach it. I discoursed on hundreds of subjects through classes I taught in Washington DC.

Next, I discovered the Kryon channelings by Lee Carroll. I purchased and studied all of his books and attended several of his workshops. Witnessing him in trance while channeling, I was astounded by his incredible font of knowledge. I learned a lot from my predecessors. I knew I could not continue to receive without giving back. Even though I was constantly teaching small groups, I realized that I could do more to reach a larger population, so I began writings books.

* * * * *

It took me 10 years to write my first book, **_A Passion for Living, a path to meaning and joy._** It was a labor of love. I would handwrite my thoughts on paper, then my wife would type it up on a typewriter. Every time I needed to update or change anything, she would retype it. It was a daunting project. I do not know how she had the patience and dedication to do it. Additionally, it was very costly. I was paying $20 per page for editing while I was still changing and updating my written material. I was inexperienced using primitive tools.

By the time I wrote my next book, **_Listening to the Voice Within, becoming enlightened_**, personal computers and word processors were common. I employed them and achieved my goal at a much faster pace.

At no time would I consider myself to be a writer. Even though this is my 6th book, I still do not consider myself to be a writer. This is because I know that on my own, I cannot write any books. I cannot take full credit for any of my books because the material was inspired.

Without inspiration, there would not be a single book of mine on the market. Often, I did not know what the book should contain or how a topic could be explained. I would seek, ask and knock just as Christ said I should and the answer would appear, often in a flash, while in bed or while walking. As soon as I had the answer, I would write it down. There were times when I would sleep apart from wife because of the numerous times I would get up in the middle of the night to write my thoughts down. At times, I would get up every few minutes for I believed that if I did not get up and write the material down, I would regret it and my inner self would stop inspiring me.

The more I responded to inspiration, the better I became at being inspired. My book, **The Secret Teachings of Christ based on the parables**, was the fastest book that I have written. The initial writing took only 1 month. Another month of editing by my wife and a third month for perfecting the material. On my own I could never do that. I am not a literary person. What I am good at, is listening to the Voice Within for inspiration.

Here are the books that I have written via inspiration so far. All are available at Amazon.com. You can search Amazon by entering my full name, Shahan Shammas.

1. A Passion for Living, a path to meaning and joy
2. Listening to the Voice Within, becoming enlightened
3. Mystery Solved! human immortality revealed
4. Know Yourself, Love Yourself, Express Yourself,

an inspiring guide to intentional living
5. The Secret Teachings of Christ, based on the parables

These books contain all of the inspirational material that I have received so far, what I have learned through the years, and what I have personally experienced and discovered. They are a treasure trove of insights, revelations and empowering knowledge. If knowledge is the basis of true and lasting power, the knowledge contained in these books will make one wise, peaceful, content, fearless, humble, compassionate and enlightened. The best investment we can ever make is the investment in ourselves. The best use we can make of our time is to dedicate some of it to the cultivation of our minds and the nurturing of our souls.

At the end of this book, I will provide you with a description of what is in each book.

* * * * *

So, how do we go about proving whether or not the soul is real, who will keep his/her soul and who will not?

First, we must know what the soul is.

I have written a book describing the soul in detail, ***Mystery Solved! human immortality revealed***. The details of this book are described later in this book.

Briefly, the soul is that aspect of God that is within us at our core. It is our I AM. It is what was "breathed" into us to make us a living soul. It is a spark, a bundle of potential. It is who we are. It is what Christ referred to as the Kingdom of God Within us. He compared it to a mustard seed, a pearl, a treasure, yeast and a net. Why these and what they stand for is explained in detail in my book, ***The Secret Teachings of Christ**, based on the parables.*

The soul *is* immortal because it is an aspect of God. Therefore, those with a soul are immortal. However, to be immortal and not know it is as good as not being immortal. It is like having a million dollars in the bank and never using it. We can only become aware of our immortality if we have a well-developed epi-soul.

We can never know of the existence of the soul by pure reason, analysis or other people's accounts. These only take us so far and is not true knowing. Unless we experience the soul ourselves, we cannot know its reality.

To understand is not the same as to know. Knowing is much more intimate if that knowledge gets incorporated within us as an aspect our personality. This requires us to go beyond understanding. We must know it in our guts. We must experience it as an undisputed reality.

If we have not experienced ourselves as soul before, then there is an alternative way to discover whether or not the soul exists. We can study its attributes and examine other people's experiences that point to the existence of the soul.

What follows are what I have experienced and demonstrated to my own satisfaction. I urge you to evaluate your own experiences and see how many proofs you can come up with that will satisfy you beyond any shadow of a doubt. Do not take anyone else's word for it. If something is important, demonstrate it to yourself before you reject it as false or accept it as a fact.

Anyone who has had any of these experiences personally, (as described in Part II) or is imbued with the attributes of the soul, (as described in Part IV) has a soul. Anyone lacking these experiences or any attribute of the soul at the end of their life, will lose his/her soul. When their bodies die, they are gone forever and erased from the book of life unless preventive action is taken now while they still live.

Even though we all have the spark, the potential and the seed for soul, it will not take root and will not manifest unless it is nurtured, tended to and developed. In other words, whether or not we end up with a soul is entirely up to us. Only if it is developed enough can we ensure our immortality. As I explain in several of my books, **the purpose of living is to cultivate our soul to progressively attain** *conscious immortality.*

PART II

EXPERIENCES

OUT-OF-BODY EXPERIENCE (OBE)

...all projections of consciousness are indeed movements by the self from one place to another, from one dimension to another, and even though the physical body may not seem to move, it is nevertheless deeply affected by these journeys. Moreover, these journeys are not only powerful inner actions that can allow a person to escape the physical dimension and work through a great deal of repression and personal dis-balance, these real journeys provide access to a pool of knowledge and power that is staggering in its magnitude.
Indeed, the most staggering of these possibilities is the energetic fact that we are indeed far more than the physical body, and that thanks to the non-physical aspects of our whole being, we have the possibility of surviving physical death!" — *John Kreiter*

One of the best ways to prove the existence of the soul is to experience it out of the body. If we have an out-of-body experience (OBE), then we know for sure that we not only have a soul, but that we are our soul. An OBE is not a theory. It is not a belief. It is knowing beyond any shadow of a doubt. Many people have had OBEs. You can have one, too. There are many books that describe techniques to achieve an OBE. I have had several OBEs. I describe some of them in detail in some of my books. Once you have an OBE experience, your doubts will vanish just as darkness is dispelled when light shines. You will know and you will be transformed.

OBEs can happen spontaneously, during sleep or as a result of trauma. Certain drugs can cause an OBE to occur as well. According to the internet, about 10% of the population have experienced an OBE.

According to Dr. Elizabeth Kubler-Ross, children near death prepare for their transition by having several OBEs. They encounter departed loved ones who are ready to help their transitioning, ease their fear and provide guidance.

NEAR-DEATH EXPERIENCE (NDE)

We tend to take a great deal for granted, because you feel like you're going to live forever. It's only if you lose a friend, or maybe have a near-death experience, [that] many events and people in your life suddenly attain real significance. – Brandon Lee

A near-death-experience (NDE) is the ultimate Out-of-Body Experience. Those who have had an NDE know the absolute reality of their souls. They have no fear of death because they know that they do not really die for they are eternal souls. Even though you might not have had an NDE, you can talk to someone, or read the account of someone, who has had an NDE and learn from his or her experience. I too have had an NDE. This experience changed my life. I describe my NDE in great detail in my book, ***A Passion for Living, a path to meaning and joy.***

An NDE is not the same as an OBE. It is much rarer and is much more impactful. One might forget the details of an OBE, but one will never forget an NDE. In an NDE, one experiences exactly what one would go through when one actually dies. However, in the case of NDEs, individuals return to their bodies. When they do, they often are aware of a mission they need to perform and they totally shed their fear of death. They become more joyous, appreciative and focused.

People experience NDEs during horrific accidents, cardiac arrest or as a result of major traumas. Patients undergoing complicated surgeries are also known to have an NDE. When they come back, they recount their experiences in detail.

According to Dr. Elizabeth Kubler-Ross, during an NDE, the soul separates from the body and is experienced as an ethereal body. The following are some of the common experiences of people undergoing an NDE:

- Complete sense of freedom;
- Absence of any panic, fear or anxiety;
- The ethereal body is always whole, no missing parts. Amputees will have their missing limbs, the blind will see and the deaf will hear;
- The dying person will be in the company of loved ones;
- The individual will be attracted to a source of bright light;
- Transition will occur through a tunnel or a bridge;
- The knowing that one is loved and cared for;
- Preservation of their identity.

SOUL VISITATIONS

A mother's arms are more comforting than anyone else's. – Princess Diana

Wouldn't it be great if a departed soul visited us personally? Wouldn't that be proof enough that the soul does indeed survive death? I have had such an experience. My mother visited me after she died when I was in the monastery in Zahle, Lebanon. Her visit left no doubt in my mind of the validity of the soul and its continued existence after death. I describe my mother's visit in my book, **_A Passion for Living_**, **_a path to meaning and joy._**

Dr. Elizabeth Kubler-Ross has personally experienced a soul visitation. A patient she cared for visited her after she had been dead. The details are in her book, **_On Life After Death_**.

People have conducted séances attempting to conjure up friendly souls. People have also used the Weija board to be influenced by spirits. There is an instance in the Bible that I referred to in one of my books where a king wanted to appeal to a prophet so he asked a woman to call up the departed spirit of the prophet to consult with.

There are many instances of spirits in the Old Testament and also in the New Testament where Christ expels them out of people.

Here are a few examples:

Old Testament:

> Now the Spirit of the LORD had turned away from Saul, and an evil spirit from the LORD tormented him. 1Sam 16:14

Calling Forth a Departed Soul

> So Saul inquired of the LORD, but the LORD did not answer him – not by dreams nor by Urim nor by the prophets. So Saul instructed his servants, "Find me a woman who is a medium, so that I may go to her and inquire of her." His servants replied to him, "There is a woman who is a medium in En Dor." So Saul disguised himself and put on other clothing and left, accompanied by two of his men. They came to the woman at night and said, "Use your ritual pit to conjure up for me the one I tell you." But the woman said to him, "Look, you are aware of what Saul has done; he has removed the mediums and magicians from the land! Why are you trapping me so you can put me to death?" But Saul swore an oath to her by the LORD, "As surely as the LORD lives, you will not incur guilt in this matter!" The woman replied, "Who is it that I should bring up for you?" He said, "Bring up for me Samuel." When the woman saw

Samuel, she cried out loudly.- The woman said to Saul, "Why have you deceived me? You are Saul!" The king said to her, "Don't be afraid! What have you seen?" The woman replied to Saul, "I have seen a divine spirit coming up from the ground!" He said to her, "What about his appearance?" She said, "An old man is coming up! He is wrapped in a robe!" Then Saul realized it was Samuel, and he bowed his face toward the ground and kneeled down. Samuel said to Saul, "Why have you disturbed me by bringing me up?" Saul replied, "I am terribly troubled! The Philistines are fighting against me and God has turned away from me. He does not answer me anymore – not by the prophets nor by dreams. So I have called on you to tell me what I should do." Samuel said, "Why are you asking me, now that the LORD has turned away from you and has become your enemy? The LORD has done exactly as I prophesied! The LORD has torn the kingdom from your hand and has given it to your neighbor David! Since you did not obey the LORD and did not carry out his fierce anger against the Amalekites, the LORD has done this thing to you today. The LORD will hand you and Israel over to the Philistines! Tomorrow both you and your sons will be with me. The LORD will also hand the army of Israel over to the Philistines!" 1 Sam 28:6-21

New Testament:

Then was Jesus led up of the Spirit into the wilderness to be tempted of the devil. Matt 4:1

If spirits exist, so does the soul since the soul is spirit.

I believe that once souls depart, they mind their own business. All indications are that as soon as a person dies, the soul leaves the body. The departed soul hangs around for a while, perhaps until their funeral is over. From my experience, I know that they can see and hear us, yet, they are unable to communicate with us. We cannot hear them or see them. Frustrated that they cannot reach us, they depart to the astral or the spiritual planes.

ANSWERS TO PRAYERS

Sometimes I thank God for unanswered prayers. Remember when you're talkin' to the man upstairs; that just because he doesn't answer doesn't mean he don't care. Some of God's greatest gifts are unanswered prayers – Garth Brooks

Even though answers to prayers are not a direct indication of the existence of the soul, they are pointers, never-the-less. If there is a power that can hear and answer our prayers, then the spirit world is real and if it is, then our spirit is part of that world.

Have any of your prayers been answered in an unequivocal way? Did you ever ask God for something in particular and know right away that your request had been granted? I have. I asked God to guide me to my soul mate, life partner, and future spouse. I was. I describe the full details of this experience in my book, **_A Passion for Living_**, **_a path to meaning and joy._** If we can be certain that our prayers are heard, then we can be certain that we are watched over and cared for by a Higher Being, a spiritual entity. The Good News is that God is our Father or Parent and we are the child or the offspring. Our nature is in the image and likeness of our Source. If God exists as spirit, so do we. If God is eternal, so are we. Just as a seed is in the image of the plant it came from, we are in the image of our Source. If our Source is "spirit" and eternal, so are we.

First, we must clearly know who we are. If we believe that we are only our bodies, then when we die, we are no more. Our bodies disintegrate and revert back to their original components—earth to earth, dust to dust. If, on the other hand, we believe ourselves to be a living soul, then that is who we are.

Please refer to my book ***Know Yourself, Love Yourself, Express Yourself**, an inspiring guide for intentional living* to find out who we are, why we are here and how to best express ourselves.

DREAMS

All that we see or seem is but a dream within a dream. – Edgar Allan Poe

Dreams can be puzzling. They can be enlightening or trivial. They can even be prophetic.

Christina Noble, a simple Irish woman who in a prophetic dream, saw the plight of Vietnamese children, their hopelessness, suffering and their need for a helping hand. She went to Vietnam and dedicated her life to serving their needs.

Here is a short write-up about her in Wikipedia:

> *In 1989, after her own children became adults, she visited Vietnam and began to care for homeless children. This action was inspired by a recurring dream she had during the Vietnam War. This eventually led her to create the Christina Noble Children's Foundation. To date, she and the Foundation have helped over 700,000 children in Vietnam and Mongolia.*

All because of a dream. Where did this dream come from? Her Higher Self, or soul, of course.

I have been investigating the nature of dreams for a long time. In almost every book of mine, I write about dreams and their significance, especially what we can learn from our dreams.

Have you ever wondered why we dream? Are dreams random activities of the brain, or are they a reflection of a far greater reality than what is apparent? Dreams are complex and simple explanations cannot do them justice. If we write down our dreams and keep a dream journal for a long time, we will come to realize that dreams are the way our inner self, our deeper reality, our soul, communicates with us symbolically. If we keep a journal and study our dreams, we will be amazed. We will know that we are of two worlds: Heaven (Soul) and Earth (Body), Light (Soul) and Darkness (Body). While soul is eternal, the body is temporary. While we are in the body, we are temporary, confined and always changing. Out of the body, we are a living soul, limitless and eternal.

The dream environment is a prelude to how it will be after we die. Just as we are unencumbered by a physical body in our dreams, this is how it will be after we leave our bodies once we die. We will be free spirits responsive only to our thoughts, desires and intentions.

WHY ATTRACTION?

The predominant thought or the mental attitude is the magnet, and the law is that like attracts like, consequently, the mental attitude will invariably attract such conditions as correspond to its nature. – Charles F. Haanel

Why are we attracted to some people and not others? If attraction is physical and purely biological, which at times it is, why the specificity? If we walk into a room full of people we have never met before, why is it that we might feel strong attraction to one or two, strong repulsion toward a few and indifference toward most? What governs our attractions and repulsions? If it were a mere biological function, how can we explain the specificity? Why do we feel comfortable with some people but not others? Obviously, we do not get attracted to the most beautiful or repulsed by the ugliest. We each have our specific tastes. What governs our attractions/repulsions? Why do we gravitate toward specific people, places, cultures, foods and even religions? Is it simply biology or is it the memory of our soul? Is it possible that our memory does not start at conception? Is it possible that we have lived before? If we did, is not that proof that we have an incarnating aspect that transcends death? This aspect is the soul.

Where do unexplained phobias come from?

I know an individual who is terrified of sharp objects, especially swords and knives. She cannot watch anyone being stabbed in movies. She has no current history of being stabbed.

I know an individual who loved a European country from his childhood without ever being there. I know Americans who prefer Orientals and end up marrying them.

Why do some individuals love reptiles such as snakes while others fear them?

Could it be that we are born with intrinsic memories from previous lives?

We are told that "an unexamined life is not worth living." If we examine carefully who our best friends are, how and why we chose them, we come to realize that it was not random.

If we examine who we marry and think deeply about what made us decide on our spouse, we will discover that it was anything but random.

Even our siblings, parents and relatives are not randomly placed in our lives. Our Inner Spiritual Self is aware of our needs and provides opportunities for life lessons we need to learn and master.

And what are some of these life lessons that we need to learn and master? According to Kryon (Lee Carroll), they are:

1. Learn to love.

2. Learn to listen.
3. Learn to receive.
4. Learn to love yourself.
5. Learn to speak your truth.
6. Learn not to be a victim.
7. Learn not to let anyone define you.
8. Learn how to feel your own mastery.
9. Learn how to live with others.
10. Learn how to get out of blaming others.
11. Learn how to drop your karma.
12. Learn how to take care of yourself more than others.
13. Learn that you deserve to be here and that you are not dirty when you are born.

The best way to know ourselves is to examine our likes, dislikes, our attractions, our fears and our passions. They are pointers to where we have been and what we have gone through and these are not limited to this one lifetime only.

HYPNOTHERAPY

The collective dream is the hypnosis of social conditioning. Only sages, psychotics & geniuses manage to break free. – Deepak Chopra

Hypnosis is a state of deep relaxation with an enhanced capacity to respond to suggestion. It might have started with the ancient Egyptians and the Greeks and was practiced by Mesmer and early European psychologists. Shamans who could enter a state of trance were practicing self-induced hypnosis.

Hypnosis is used to overcome undesirable habits such as smoking, to retrieve forgotten information from the subconscious and to discover the cause of phobias and diseases. Some hypnotherapists, such as Dolores Cannon, have discovered that, while accessing the subconscious, they can retrieve information about the patient's past lives. These practitioners often did not believe in reincarnation or past lives when they first began conducting their hypnotic regressions.

Dolores Cannon discovered past lives by accident. After witnessing patients go into past lives for over 50 years, she became a staunch believer in reincarnation and past life therapy.

Here is a short quote form her author bio:

> *"Having conducted sessions with thousands of clients, recording the same results time and time again and spending vast amounts of time and energy verifying the authenticity of her clients" past lives, Dolores was able to decisively conclude that her results were indeed genuine and that she had tapped into an incredibly powerful source of information. As she explored further, she gradually became aware that the information she was receiving about past lives, different periods in time and a variety of other topics were not actually coming from the conscious minds of the clients she was hypnotizing."* Dolores Cannon website

The information was coming from the subconscious of her patients. Dolores Cannon has written 17 books. Almost all of her patients recount past life experiences. If thousands of individuals experience past lives while under hypnosis and deep trance, there must be something to it.

If reincarnation is a fact, which I believe it is, then the reality of the soul cannot be disputed. If we have lived before, then we will live again.

Hypnotherapy, reincarnation and past lives are more indicators of the reality of the soul.

BIOLOGY

We are survival machines – robot vehicles blindly programmed to preserve the selfish molecules known as genes. This is a truth which still fills me with astonishment. – Richard Dawkins

We are told that environment and heredity determine individuality, but these two factors alone do not adequately explain differences in people. Family members often share a great deal of heredity and environment, yet exhibit distinct personality traits. Two children born to the same parents and living under similar circumstances can exhibit incredibly different traits and personalities. I believe that a third factor is required to explain differences in people. This third contributor is "soul personality", or epi-soul. Soul personality is what we build in each life time. It contains our accumulated experiences and the memories of lessons learned. Deep inside, we know that we are more than genetics and environment. We are a soul personality with inherited memories, talents and abilities from many past lives.

The theory of reincarnation has been around for a very long time. It is taught by many religions, including early

Christianity, and believed by millions of people the world over. I do not want to discourse at length about the validity of this belief. I hope you will look into it as another proof of the existence of the soul. There are many who actually remember some of their past incarnations. There are hundreds of books written on this subject. Please consider it as another window that opens up the possibility that the soul is real.

SELF-SACRIFICE

A human being has many divine qualities. But there has never been another unparalleled divine quality like man's self-sacrifice, nor can there ever be. – Sri Chinmoy

If the theory of Natural Selection and Survival of the Fittest was adequate to explain the nature of human evolution, then how can we explain acts of heroism and self-sacrifice? Individuals sacrifice their lives for the benefit of others because deep down they know that their lives do not end with death. If death were the end of it all, we would have been biologically prevented from sacrificing our lives for others. The knowledge that death is not the end comes from deep within. It is intrinsic. The validity of the soul is self-evident when we spring into action to save another. It is also evident during meditation when we are alone, quiet and reflective.

One of the earliest examples of self-sacrifice that I remember is in the story ***A Tale of Two Cities*** by Charles Dickens, published in 1859. People deeply in love do not hesitate to sacrifice for their beloved. Loving mothers would never hesitate to sacrifice their life for their children. Christianity teaches that God loves us so much that He was willing to sacrifice His only begotten Son to save us.

I recall an example of self-sacrifice in Washington DC when a plane crashed on takeoff and plunged into the Potomac in the dead of winter. A man threw himself into the water in an attempt to rescue others. He drowned in the process.

If we did not know in our hearts, that we live on after our physical death, we would not sacrifice ourselves. We would be biologically prevented from sacrificing ourselves. The soul and its survival must be real for self-sacrifices to take place.

THE CHANGELESS

You are the only one of you. From the beginning of time till the end of this world to the end of eternity. There's only one of you ever created. Ev-er. You are the only you. That's pretty powerful. So why on earth would you want to look like anybody else, dress like anyone else, dance like anyone else, be someone else, when you are a legend in your own right? – Mia Michaels

Even though our bodies have been changing since conception, and our emotions and mental states have been maturing, there is a permanent aspect to our being. We always know who we are. There is continuity to our being. Our individuality, our uniqueness, and our sense of identity are never in doubt. Even though our cells die and new ones are born and the atoms composing our bodies are completely replaced every few years, we always know who we are regardless of any changes that we go through. Our essence is always the same. It remains changeless, ageless and inviolate. This changeless essence is the soul in the form of our I AM.

In my book ***Know Yourself, Love Yourself, Express Yourself,*** I explain that we have astral and spiritual bodies in addition to our physical body. Yet, the only permanent aspect of our being is our I AM. It alone is changeless. I explain that the astral body must evolve into the spiritual body and the spiritual body's ultimate goal is to merge with the I AM.

The I AM is the Source of our soul which is in two parts: original spark as soul which is the same for everyone and a cultivated aspect of the soul, the epi-soul, which is unique to each individual. It is the epi-soul that allows us to experience conscious immortality. In other words, unless we have a well-developed epi-soul we will never remember or know of our immortality.

A TEST

The intuitive mind is a sacred gift and the rational mind is a faithful servant. We have created a society that honors the servant and has forgotten the gift. – Albert Einstein

Have you ever told yourself that you wanted to wake up at a certain time and sure enough you wake up at exactly the time you specified? I have done this on numerous occasions. How is this possible? If this is a function of the brain, how can the brain tell conventional time? I know the body has a biological clock but this is not the same as the ordinary clock that we have on the wall. We must have something that is beyond the body that complies with our intentions. There must be an aspect of us that is awake while we sleep. This aspect cannot be bound by the body, for conventional time is not in the body. We created conventional time to measure duration. What is this aspect that can wake us up at the exact time we want to wake up? We can call it whatever we like, but its reality remains the same. I attribute this aspect to our Higher Self, an aspect of our soul.

Similarly, we might know who is calling us before we check it out.

We might know of a letter we will be receiving.

Many have gut feelings that turn out to be accurate.

Many have insights about individuals on first contact that turn out to be correct.

Many have a highly developed Extra-Sensory Perception (ESP).

I know spouses who can read each other's minds.

We must have something that transcends the limitations of space and time. We do. It is our soul.

SYNCHRONICITY

In every moment, the Universe is whispering to you. You're constantly surrounded by signs, coincidences, and synchronicities, all aimed at propelling you in the direction of your destiny. – Denise Linn

I owe my life to synchronicity. I could write a book about my experiences with synchronicities. Synchronicity is not only what happens that is surprising, it is also what does not happen that should have happened. I attribute two of my incredible synchronicities that led to transformative changes in my life to two failures that should not have taken place. In retrospect, I am glad they did. My failures turned out to be fortunate indeed. My failures were doorways that led me to much greener pastures.

What is synchronicity. how and why does it happen?

> *Synchronicity is a concept introduced by Carl Jung, founder of analytical psychology, to describe events that coincide in time and appear meaningfully related, yet lack a discoverable causal connection. Jung held that this was a healthy function of the mind, although it can*

become harmful within psychosis. Wikipedia

Since all of my synchronicities were to my advantage, they must be premeditated and planned. My conscious mind had no part in planning these synchronicities. If they were not planned by me, then by who? Since they are so numerous in my life and almost impossible to arrange consciously by myself, how and why do they happen?

In several of my books I refer to the Higher Self which is an aspect of the soul. If we have an awakened Higher Self, then we have a well-developed epi-soul and if we have a well-developed epi-soul, then we must definitely have a soul.

Synchronicities are arranged by our Higher Self, an aspect of our soul, to place us on an accelerated path to unfold our potential and manifest our destiny.

PART III

THE SUBLIME

THE SUBLIME

To experience sublime natural beauty is to confront the total inadequacy of language to describe what you see. Words cannot convey the scale of a view that is so stunning it is felt. – Eleanor Catton

It was in the monastery that I came to reject the god of the Old Testament, a god of judgment, jealousy, anger, vengeance and favoritism. I do not believe in fearing or in worshiping such a god. Yet, I do believe in God, albeit, a different kind of a God.

As I began to write my books, I discovered a God I can love, believe in and worship. This God is a trinity of **_Love, Beauty and Joy_**. Since we are in the image of this God, likewise our essence, or soul is Love, Beauty and Joy. We are not in the image of God as a physical body, but rather as who we are – a soul personality. It is only our soul that is in the image of God, hence it is a trinity of Love, Beauty and Joy.

This simplifies knowing whether or not we have a soul. Anyone who knows, experiences and exudes Love, Beauty and Joy has a soul.

Have you ever listened to a song, read a poem or a book and were touched to your core? Have you ever watched a movie or listened to a story and were overwhelmed by emotion? If you have, then you have experienced the sublime. There are two distinct experiences we can have: the ordinary and the transcendent (sublime). While the body experiences emotions such as pain and pleasure, fear and anger, all of which are ordinary, the soul experiences Joy, Beauty and Divine Love, all of which are sublime.

We seem to be biologically wired to experience the sublime. We are born into and live with a sense of connectedness to the sublime and to a reality higher than our individual self. This sense of the sublime comes from the depth of our being. It is the yearning of our soul to connect with a reality beyond the physical, a reality that is our Source and essence. This reality manifests in moments of inspiration and insight and when we are taken over by Love, intoxicated by Beauty and overwhelmed by Joy. In my book, **A Passion for Living**, *a path to meaning and joy,* I describe a simple experience I once had eating an ordinary garden tomato that turned out not to be ordinary at all. This sublime experience transformed my understanding of the connectedness of life. I would like to share that experience here with you.

The TOMATO

I picked a tomato from my garden and looked at it. I did not look at it casually, but with a deep desire to really ***know*** *what is this thing we call a tomato?!*

I remember planting the seed. Then, after an ambiguous period of not knowing what was taking place in the soil, I saw a tiny seedling break the surface of the soil. It was as if it was declaring silently but resolutely **"I am here and I am alive!"** The plant grew in width and height until it became fully mature. It acquired many stems, branches and leaves and even though I could not see the roots, I knew they were there. Then many tiny yellow flowers formed beside the leaves on the stems.

After a few days, I saw tiny bulbous structures at the base of the flowers. At first small, hard and green, they grew to become large, soft and red.

I now hold one of them in my hand and look at it attentively, curiously and lovingly. What are you?

Red, soft and round.

The colors green and red displayed by you are not inherent in you. Color is due to light, absorption, refraction and the structures of my eyes and brain. At night, your color is not there, for it never was in you even when I saw it there. What I see as color is what you do not absorb when the rays of light reach you. You reflect the color I see. What you reject, I consider an essential aspect of you. What I see tells me as much about me as it does about you.

I cannot know how hard or soft you are until I touch you. By touching you, my own structure, my nervous system and how it functions, are revealed to me. I interpret my own sensations, thoughts and ideas as qualities of yours.

Looking at you when you were round, but small and green, I could not understand how you would be able to slowly transform yourself into a much larger round structure with a different color—red. I could see you getting larger on a daily basis. Even though, logically, I understand how you do that, I still do not fully realize the magic unfolding before my eyes.

I am told that you are a bunch of cells grouped together in a specific way. But these cells are not the same cells that formed you a while ago. When you were a tiny bulbous structure you had very few cells compared to now. How did you know how to create all these extra cells and add them to yourself? I am told that you are constantly changing and that you have been adding to yourself from the soil, the air and the sun. If life progresses only from life, how could the soil, the water, the air and the sun add to your body and life? How can you take inert elements and give life to them? Or, are all these elements and the sunshine alive as well?

Your journey from a tiny, green, knot-like structure until you became the red, soft and large tomato I now hold and observe, lasted about four weeks. During this journey, you constantly changed your features while extending in the three dimensions of space. During this time, you were also extending in the fourth dimension of time. Your journey appears to have started from when you were tiny, green and knot-like, but for your journey to begin the plant had to be first. For the plant to be, the soil, seed, water and sunshine had to be first. Where is the real beginning?! All beginnings and endings are mere apparent starts and ends. Since you are always in a state of change, your journey is ongoing. Your beginning with me was the seed I planted. That seed had to come from somewhere. It had its own journey. Your seeds and cells will have their own journeys as well. In a way, you had no true beginning and are not going to have an ultimate end. The cells that formed you were part of some other structures. Now they are going to be part of another. Before I picked you up, you were part of the plant. To remind me of your previous connection, you carry a "scar" the same way that I carry a belly button to remind me and others of my previous connection. The same way that I came from my mother, you came from your mother —the plant. The plant is connected to the soil just as you were connected to the plant. The soil, in turn, is connected to earth. Earth is connected to the solar system. The solar system is connected to the galaxies and the universe.

Where does it all end or start? Your atoms and cells, just like mine, are always combining, breaking down and recombining. Since nothing can be created nor destroyed, all that now is, has always been, only in different combinations, assuming different forms and existing in diverse spaces and times.

I look at you again. What makes you now must have been a part of everything else, at one time or another; from the beginning, now and forever.

Behold, when I look at you, I see eternity.

Slowly I lift the tomato up and bring it closer to me. Now it is seen as separate and apart, as a tomato. I open my mouth and reverently consume the tomato. It is now part of me. The eternity that was the tomato is now part of the eternity that is me. The journey continues. What constituted the tomato is now breaking down. The particles of the tomato will recombine and reappear in a different form. They will no more be known as a tomato, or seen apart by themselves. Henceforth, the particles will be called by a new name. They will take on my identity and the journey will go on until I, too, am dissolved, absorbed and recombined into other forms. Then, I too will appear in a different garment and be known by a new name.

I take a long and deep breath.

What is true of the tomato is equally true of the air I just breathed in and the sun whose rays are shining upon me. Soil, air and sunshine forming the tomato; tomato, air and sunshine forming me.

I am always becoming with everything else. Is air part of me? Is water or food part of me? They are not until I take them in and then they are.

How can I be so dependent on these elements and yet proclaim a separate existence? This is the paradox of the ages. I am, yet without all else, I cannot be.

Can I have a body without what I consume? Can I have emotions without others to interact with and an environment to respond to? How can I depend so much on others to stimulate and cause my emotions and yet think that I have a separate existence of my own? Is not my intelligence activated and developed as a response to my environment? Did not my senses form as a result of being in this world, immersed in earthly experiences?

I am in the image of my environment and my environment is in my image. Environment and I, like chicken and egg, have always existed and coexist. We both assume various garbs, colors, shapes and form numerous associations. We take on unique identities for a while and then exchange them for new ones. As we exchange, we change. We give birth to our new selves.

__A Passion for Living__, a path to meaning and joy

PART IV

ATTRIBUTES

Primary Attributes
    1. Love
    2. Beauty
    3. Joy

Secondary Attributes
    1. Inspiration
    2. Imagination, Visualization, Creativity
    3. Sympathy, Empathy, Compassion
    4. Service
    5. Forgiveness
    6. Character and Personality

LOVE

One day you will ask me which is more important? My life or yours? I will say mine and you will walk away not knowing that you are my life. – Khalil Gibran

When we say God is Love, this love is a unique form of love. It is not lust, desire or passion. It is spiritual—a pure, unselfish outpouring of compassion. It is unconditional in that we are loved regardless of who we are, what we have done or did not do. This is how God (our Source) loves us. This love is beyond measure.

God loves us because we are an outpouring of His nature. When a mother loves a newborn, it is because she knows this baby is an outpouring from her. A mother loves her baby unconditionally. This is spiritual love with no strings attached.

Few know this form of love. Once we are touched by the fire of this love, we can never un-love regardless of what an individual does, did or did not do. It is permanent. Not only that, it grows over time and it becomes more established and harder to dismiss.

Love is a glue that holds the universe together. It is the affinity between atoms, elements, cells, tissues, organs and systems. Our soul is of the nature of His love. It holds the elements of our body together.

Love is a one-way street. It is a pouring out, a giving without end.

This love does not need a reason to love. There is no why as to the love. Love is its nature.

This love is all-consuming, all-pervading and transformative. It transmutes the lover and the loved.

Love is the first aspect of the nature of God and the soul. Experiencing love is witnessing soul and God in action.

BEAUTY

Beauty, the splendour of truth, is a gracious presence when the imagination contemplates intensely the truth of its own being or the visible world, and the spirit which proceeds out of truth and beauty is the holy spirit of joy. These are realities and these alone give and sustain life. −James Joyce

What is beauty?

We know beauty when we see it.

We know beauty when we hear it.

We know beauty when it touches our soul.

They say that beauty is symmetry. Perhaps. But there is beauty in a multiplicity of forms all having diverse symmetries.

Beauty has a life of its own. It radiates life. It announces itself. It pulls you into itself and it transforms you.

Have you ever been "struck" by beauty? I have, more than once.

Beauty is stunning. It is like electricity. It can zap you.

If you can be moved by beauty, not only are you alive, but so is your soul. The easier one is touched by beauty, the more developed the epi-soul is. In other words, being touched by beauty is a sure indication that one has a well-developed soul.

The most mature soul finds beauty everywhere and in everything including what we term the ugly.

Beauty is the second aspect of the nature of God and soul. Experiencing beauty is witnessing soul and God in action.

JOY

We need Joy as we need air. We need Love as we need water. We need each other as we need the earth we share. – Maya Angelou

By exuding love, finding and appreciating beauty everywhere, we are automatically in a state of joy or bliss. Joy is not something we pursue. It is what happens when we love deeply, unselfishly and spiritually.

Joy is different from pleasure. While pleasure is derived, is temporary and often local, joy happens. It takes over. It engulfs. Joy is the result of being in love with beauty.

I would like to quote a few appropriate passages from my first book, A ***Passion for Living, a path to meaning and joy***:

> Savor every stage in your life and every role you get to play. When you are a spouse, a parent, a student, or a laborer, be the best you can be for this is your moment in history to demonstrate what you can do in each situation. We are actors and actresses in our current role. This is our opportunity to stamp the event with our uniqueness. We go through each stage

of our lives once and for a short duration. If we learn to appreciate whatever comes our way and take full advantage of our opportunities to make a positive contribution, then what we can enjoy and cherish is limited only by our imagination.

There is nothing commonplace in life. There are only common eyes. Even a "common" activity such as talking, walking, or cooking is magical. When we see and experience magic everywhere, we carry that sense of wonder with us. We become transformed and our lives become filled with peace, joy and gratitude. Living becomes sacred.

The greatest power we have to shape our lives is the power to think, feel and act with awareness and intent. Through these we can sculpt our lives and fashion our circumstances.

We must not wait for grand events to make us happy. Rather, we should celebrate each moment with a spirit of gratefulness for the gifts of life. Being thankful is a vitamin that aides our health and hastens our blossoming. To assist us in this process, we can make a list of items for which we are grateful, beginning with being alive, having family and friends.

Possessions and "things" cannot give us joy. They can make us happy and give us pleasure temporarily. They can also make us sad and miserable. This is because "things" have different values and meaning to different people at different times. If we have never tasted a perfectly ripe fruit such as a banana, a mango or a peach, then the first few times we savor them and derive pleasure from the experience. For someone who grew up on a farm eating fruit on an ongoing basis, that same experience is mundane. When something is new, we appreciate and value it more. Once it gets old, it loses its significance. Many base their happiness, or lack of, on possessions. Possessions, just like happiness and misery, are temporary and fickle. Instead, we should seek the permanent in the form of joy.

Happiness and misery are mental states. They are predicated upon our memories, our expectations and our anticipation. Once we master mental alchemy, we derive pleasure and joy from anything. We can learn to see beauty anywhere and fall in love with the ordinary, because there is nothing ordinary in life, only ordinary eyes, ears and minds.

Being in Divine Love, we see beauty everywhere and experience joy on an ongoing basis. Being in love, appreciating beauty and experiencing joy is expressing soul and manifesting God and divinity. It is expressing our true nature, a testimony to the divinity of our soul.

Joy is the third aspect of the nature of God and soul. Experiencing joy is witnessing soul and God in action.

SECONDARY ATTRIBUTES

1. Inspiration
2. Imagination, Visualization, Creativity
3. Sympathy, Empathy, Compassion
4. Service
5. Forgiveness
6. Character and Personality

INSPIRATION

Just don't give up trying to do what you really want to do. Where there is love and inspiration, I don't think you can go wrong. – Ella Fitzgerald

Have you ever been inspired? Have you ever had a strong hunch, or a gut feeling about something and you were right about it? Where did the inspiration come from? Where did this gut feeling originate from? These did not come from our brain because they are original and we could not have known of them. These came to us but not from us, at least not the normal us. Where did they come from? They came from our Inner Self or soul which is in touch with the Universal Soul, the Source or God. If we learn to listen and trust this inner "voice", we will not only live healthier, happier, prosperous and productive lives, we will be on an accelerated path to epi-soul growth and spiritual development. I have devoted an entire book to this subject titled, **Listening to the Voice Within,** *becoming enlightened.*

Inspiration is critical in my life. I depend on it. Without inspiration, I cannot write. Without inspiration, I would not have any published books. Without inspiration, I would not be able to teach. Without inspiration, I cannot function. Often, I receive the material for writing and teaching while I am in the act of writing and teaching.

How does inspiration work?

Inspiration is an idea, a thought, or an urge that lands on us. It simply appears, but it is not an intruder. It is an invited guest. We not only request it and expect to receive it; we must also prepare for it by being ready. In other words, we must be able to put the inspiration to good use when we receive it or else it does not serve any purpose.

Inspiration requires an incubation period . It is always an answer to a question, a solution to a problem or about what our next step should be.

I believe that the more developed a soul is, the easier it is to be inspired. The more we allow the Higher Spiritual Self to function through us, the more of an outpouring of inspiration we will be blessed with.

I am thankful for inspiration for without it, I would not be able to carry out the mission I undertook for myself.

CREATIVITY, IMAGINATION, VISUALIZATION

Imagination is the beginning of creation. You imagine what you desire, you will what you imagine and at last you create what you will. – George Bernard Shaw

Creativity, imagination, visualization, concentration, contemplation, meditation and effective prayer are advanced mental tools. They are a reflection of a highly developed mind which itself is an indication of an awakened and lively soul.

The soul imbues us with life, mind and consciousness. The more developed the mind and the higher our level of consciousness, the more awakened the soul is. By soul, I mean the epi-soul, the part that we can nurture and develop.

It is evident that those with a well-developed soul have a

keen mind and a higher level of consciousness. In other words, those with developed souls can use their minds and consciousness to live a life of creativity, abundance and contentment.

It is easier to attain goals when one can employ the advanced tools of the mind. Creativity, imagination and visualization are the means for innovation, breakthrough solutions and are how we attract that which we seek into our lives. Meditation and prayer are states of being that result in peace, health and contentment for those who practice it. Mastering the use of these tools is what sets people apart from each other and from beasts. These tools help transform an ordinary life into an extraordinary one.

Those who live by primitive instincts, unexamined habits and who always take the path of least resistance, live as beasts. Those who employ the advanced tools of the mind and the heart are cultivated, souled human beings.

SYMPATHY, EMPATHY AND COMPASSION

Compassion asks us to go where it hurts, to enter into the places of pain, to share in brokenness, fear, confusion, and anguish. Compassion challenges us to cry out with those in misery, to mourn with those who are lonely, to weep with those in tears. Compassion requires us to be weak with the weak, vulnerable with the vulnerable, and powerless with the powerless. Compassion means full immersion in the condition of being human. – Henri Nouwen

Sympathy, empathy and compassion are similar terms that denote the ability of an individual to step outside of themselves and be concerned with the difficulties of another and do something about them.

The Meriam-Webster dictionary defines sympathy as:

> a. *an affinity, association, or relationship between persons or things wherein whatever affects one similarly affects the other*
> b. *mutual or parallel susceptibility or a condition brought about by it*
> c. *Unity or harmony in action or effect*

While sympathy is concern for another, empathy is actively sharing in the person's emotional experience.

Compassion, on the other hand, means to suffer together. Com = together and passion = suffering. We do not need to suffer to be compassionate. Often all we need to do is show sympathy and understanding. Giving a person a hug, a loving touch or simply listening attentively without judgment is often all we need to do.

To attune to another's misery is a sign of a well-developed soul. To put oneself in another's shoes is also an indication of a mature soul. Even better, to react to the distress of another with a balm is a sure sign of a well-developed soul.

Obviously, the reverse is also true.

Those without sympathy, empathy or compassion are at the level of beasts. They have not evolved their souls yet. Selfishness, callousness and egoism are hallmarks of childishness and immaturity. Those who only think of themselves have a long way to go before they grow spiritually and mature.

The first step on the path of nurturing and caring for the soul is to stop thinking of self and focus on others instead.

We begin by cultivating the attitude of thankfulness, gratitude and appreciation for our lives as they are. Next, we step outside of ourselves and think of others. We must look for what we can do to ease other people's pain, suffering and distress.

We should constantly count our blessings. If we wake up each morning, then that is reason enough to be thankful. There are those who go to bed and never wake up. Finding reasons to be happy is conducive to our health and well-being.

By continuously expressing gratitude, we are in a constant state of prayer.

By pouring out sympathy, empathy and compassion, we water the seedling of our soul and nurture it to grow and blossom.

SERVICE

Nobody cares how much you know, until they know how much you care. – Theodore Roosevelt

It follows that when we stop thinking of ourselves and think of others, we would want to find ways to help others by serving their needs. Needs are different from wants. We want to help, but we do not want to create dependencies. We want to empower individuals to be self-sufficient. Serving the needs of others is ennobling and should be carried out anonymously without any fanfare.

It is an irony of life that the more we focus on the happiness of others, the happier we get. Making other people happy does not diminish our happiness. When we give to enrich another's life, it is spiritual giving. The Pharisee way of giving, on the other hand, does not engender happiness in the giver, just pride, ego and self-aggrandizement. Christ taught us the value of service. He also showed us the way to do it, not letting the left hand know what the right hand is doing.

We are all interdependent. We go through cycles. There was a time when my family and I needed the assistance of others. We were dependent on the charity of others. Thankfully, those days are behind us. I do not regret having gone through those experiences which at the time were humiliating and demeaning. I have learned value, developed sympathy, empathy and compassion. It was well worth it.

Christ demonstrated the value of service by washing the feet of His Disciples. We do not need to go that far. Often just by being there, smiling and by simply touching another in a loving and understanding way is all it takes.

For an enlightening exposition of the hidden meaning of the Last Supper and the washing of the feet, please refer to my book, **_The Secret Teachings of Christ_ based on the parables**.

FORGIVENESS

When we harbor negative emotions toward others or toward ourselves, or when we intentionally create pain for others, we poison our own physical and spiritual systems. By far the strongest poison to the human spirit is the inability to forgive oneself or another person. It disables a person's emotional resources. The challenge...is to refine our capacity to love others as well as ourselves and to develop the power of forgiveness. – Caroline Myss

Christ admonished us to forgive 77 times.

Then Peter came up and said to him, "Lord, how often will my brother sin against me, and I forgive him? As many as seven times?" Jesus said to him, "I do not say to you seven times, but seventy-seven times. Mat 18:2-22

The number 77 is symbolic. It denotes until perfect forgiveness is achieved. Please refer to the parables of Christ in my book, **_The Secret Teachings of Christ_ based on the parables** to understand what the hidden meaning of the numbers used by Christ reveal.

We must forgive not only others but ourselves as well. Forgiveness benefits the one forgiving more than the one being forgiven. Forgiveness is about letting go. It is like dropping a burnt match that we no longer have any use for. We should not waste our time and energy on what has already taken place. We should learn from it, make amends if the fault was ours, put it behind us and move on. Fretting over spilled milk does no one any good.

The degree of the faults we are willing to forgive is an indication of the maturity of our souls. The bigger the offense we are able to forgive, the more developed our souls are. Similarly, if we hold onto a grievance and are unable to forgive, then this is a sign of our immaturity and the smallness of our soul.

CHARACTER AND PERSONALITY

The thought manifests as the word. The word manifests as the deed. The deed develops into habit. And the habit hardens into character. So watch the thought and its ways with care. And let it spring from love, born out of concern for all beings. – Gautama Buddha

Our character and personality are a reflection of the status of where we are along the path of nurturing and developing our soul. The more patient, focused, compassionate and forgiving we are, the more developed our soul is.

Our character and personality are the product of the thoughts we entertain, the feelings we dwell on, the habits we form and the use we make of our experiences. It is true that it is not so much what happens to us that impacts us, but how we interpret our experiences and how we react to them.

Experiencing hardships is part of being human. We all

have these experiences, but we do not all learn the same way. Some of us become bitter, complain and feel sorry for ourselves; others learn from their hardships and become better as a result.

How we handle the major events of our lives is based on our character and personality. We are going to experience unanticipated tragedies and blessings. How we manage our tragedies and blessings is a matter of character. We can regulate how we feel and for how long. We can decide to be optimistic rather than pessimistic. We can choose to dwell on what we can do, instead of what we cannot do. We can starve the negative by nourishing the positive.

The greatest gift we have is freedom of choice. However, if we function from the ego, we are never free to exercise freedom of choice. Only by detaching and functioning from our Higher Spiritual Self are we free to exercise true freedom of choice.

Even though we are not fully free and are handicapped by various limitations due to heredity, environment and culture, there is a lot we can do to alter the course of our lives by making the right choices. The more we educate ourselves, the better our choices will be.

Building our character and personality is a slow process and can take lifetimes. Hence a well-developed character and personality is not only an indication of a mature soul, but also of the many incarnations that the individual had to go through to attain that level of maturity.

Character and personality are aspects of the soul. They are retained from one lifetime to the next. They are treasures that do not spoil.

PART V

UNDERSTANDING THE SOUL

1. Dimensions and Reality
2. The Composition of Soul
3. The Purpose of Life
4. A Simple Way to Experience Soul
5. Does the Soul Need to be Saved?

DIMENSIONS AND REALITY

Once I opened my eyes to the realities of life, I couldn't close them. – Emmanuelle Beart

The body is physical and three dimensional. The soul is spiritual and multidimensional. The subject of dimensions is vast and I have devoted a complete chapter in my first book, **_A Passion for Living_, _a path to meaning and joy_** describing it in detail. By understanding what the various dimensions are, we get to know our true nature. We understand, not only the nature of the soul, but also our connections to all that exists.

A basic understanding of the various dimensions will aid our comprehension of how the ONE can contain the many and remain a unit at the same time.

Simply, the first dimension is that of the line containing all points.

The second dimension is that of the plane containing all lines.

The third dimension is that of the solid containing all planes.

The fourth dimension is that of space/time containing all solids.

The fifth dimension is that of the idea containing all space/time.

The sixth dimension is that of the mind containing all ideas.

The seventh dimension is that of the Cosmic Mind, God, the Source containing all.

Anything beyond the fourth dimension is outside space and time and is unlimited and eternal.

THE COMPOSITION OF SOUL

This is the ultimate end of man, to find the One which is in him; which is his truth, which is his soul; the key with which he opens the gate of the spiritual life, the heavenly kingdom. – Rabindranath Tagore

What exactly is Soul? Soul is multidimensional and therefore eludes a simple three-dimensional definition. An easy way to understand soul, however, is to look at it as if it were a seed. Perhaps that is why Christ alluded to the Kingdom of Heaven within us as being like a mustard seed:

> *Another parable put he forth unto them, saying, The kingdom of heaven is like to a grain of mustard seed, which a man took, and sowed in his field: Which indeed is the least of all seeds: but when it is grown, it is the greatest among herbs, and becometh a tree, so that the birds of the air come and lodge in the branches thereof. Matt 13:31-32*

Our soul, too, must be nurtured, and like a seed, when it is fully grown and mature, it will be like a magnificent tree that attracts all sorts of blessings into our lives and enrich the lives of others.

The soul we start with initially is our one talent. Christ alluded to this in the Parable of the Talents. Christ explained that some are given one, others 2 while a few are given 5 talents. The ones who have 2 or more talents have been industrious in previous lives and have multiplied their initial investment. The person with one talent is a beginner. In the Parable of the Talents, the one with the one talent decided to hide his talent rather than invest it. When the master returned and found out that this servant hid his talent instead of investing it, He took it away from him and gave it to the others who had been industrious.

The parable of the talents is an allusion to the soul and free will we have been endowed with. Our talent, our soul, includes our time, skills and abilities. We must decide what to do with them. We must invest some of these to nurture and cultivate our soul. This is what is expected of us and what the main purpose of life is.

The initial soul is like a seed that has three characteristics:
1. A seed is condensed potential of its source and is in the image and likeness of its source. An apple seed, when it grows and matures will become like its source—an apple tree. A seed also has the potential to add to its inherited abilities as it experiences, grows and matures.

2. A seed is a dormant life entity. Once planted, it grows, responds to its environment and multiplies.

3. A seed has intelligence. It attracts to itself what it

needs to grow and unfold. As it grows, it begins to display the source from which it originated. While an apple seed will become an apple tree, our soul will mature and reflect the nature of its Source, God—Love, Beauty and Joy.

Similarly, souls have 3 features:

1. Souls are condensed potential in the image and likeness of their Source. Souls can manifest their potential through living and experiencing. Each soul is a unique Image, Idea, Word, and Identity that God had in mind from the beginning. As we were released from the Mind of God, we were endowed with free will to seek the manner of our unfoldment, growth and maturation. We can take the short road and be on an accelerated path, or we can take the long road. We can go either way as long as we do not stagnate and refuse to grow.

2. Souls are not only alive, but they are the life force that animates the body. They are the life of the body. The body lives while it houses the soul. The body dies as soon as the soul departs.

3. Souls have intelligence. This intelligence manifests as Consciousness, Life and Mind. Our soul will attract to us the circumstances we need to grow and mature. These are often challenges we must overcome and obstacles that we must transform into opportunities so we can gain mastery.

Our soul gives us our unique identity. It houses our character and personality. It is our spiritual DNA. Initially, as soul, it is perfect and in the image of its Source, God.

As we live and experience, we deposit on this pristine soul our accumulated memories and distort the original image into something of our own making. It reflects the choices we have made and the actions we have taken. What we add to soul is epi-soul. Over time, the original Idea, Image and Word become personalized, a reflection of us instead of God. This is because of our freedom of choice. Once we learn to make the "right" choices, our development will accelerate until we finally reflect our divine nature.

The Source of our life is the soul. Life endows us with consciousness and awareness. Hence, we remain alive for as long as our soul remains attached to the body via a "spiritual umbilical cord." When this cord snaps or is severed, either through an accident or naturally, we die.
Our soul also endows us with mind and intelligence. Mind is a tool we can use to create, fashion and design the life we choose by exercising freedom of choice. Mind is like an ocean while we are like fish in this ocean. Even though the entire ocean is available to us, we seldom venture beyond our conscious and subconscious mind. Our vast potential lies in accessing the Universal Mind—the vast ocean.

Mind consists of three subdivisions: Conscious, Subconscious and the Super Conscious or Universal Mind. The conscious mind is the tip of the iceberg. We use it in our daily lives to survive and manage in our current environment. In the beginning we lived employing instinct, intuition and impulse. As we experience and learn, we grow and mature. We acquire knowledge, understanding and wisdom. With these, we begin to use will, reason, and intention to shape our destiny.

The conscious mind is the surface of the mind while the subconscious is the deeper layer which houses our accumulated memories, habits, beliefs, fears, desires, dreams, attitudes, expectations, hopes, aspirations and intentions. The subconscious mind directs our involuntary activities. We can access our subconscious mind and alter its contents via our thoughts, feelings, intentions and actions. We do this by forming habits. By choosing the habits that we form, we create subroutines that not only simplify our lives but can keep us healthier and happier. It all starts by being selective in what thoughts we entertain, what feelings we allow and the actions we repeat until a desired habit is formed. Habits reside in the subconscious.

The subconscious mind is in direct contact with the Universal Mind. This Universal Mind is the ocean that contains all. It is what connects all the living in a web that transcends space and time. Even though we are all connected through the Universal Mind, we are seldom aware of this connection. Inspiration, revelation and The Voice Within come to us through our connection with the Universal Mind. Our Higher Spiritual Self is the gateway to the Universal Mind.

THE PURPOSE OF LIFE

If you can't figure out your purpose, figure out your passion. For your passion will lead you right into your purpose. – T. D. Jakes

What then is the purpose of life?

Simply put it is to experience, to grow and to mature. It is to progress into adulthood. This entails the full realization that we are Children of God in the image of our Source. To become mature is the same as for the Seed to become the Tree, for the Image to become Real, for the Idea to manifest as Actual and for the Word to become the Book of Life. Once we are mature, we demonstrate love for ourselves, for others, and for nature. Our eyes open and our ears clear up. We begin to SEE, FEEL, HEAR, and RELATE deeply and intimately. We live as MASTERS progressively manifesting our unique nature and inheritance. We live and act as Children of God. As we do, our epi-soul continues to grow until we attain conscious immortality by uniting with our I AM, the diving aspect of ourselves immersed in God. The Ego disappears and we become our Soul, the I AM. We reflect our Source—Love, Beauty and Joy.

A SIMPLE WAY TO EXPERIENCE SOUL

The body is only a garment. How many times you have changed your clothing in this life, yet because of this you would not say that you have changed. Similarly, when you give up this bodily dress at death you do not change. You are just the same, an immortal soul, a child of God. – Paramahansa Yogananda

We are aware of our bodies. We can see, touch and feel them. We need our bodies for our earthly experiences.

We are aware of our thoughts. We use them daily to function.

We are aware of our emotions. We need them to navigate our interactions and relationships.

To experience our soul, we need to go beyond our bodies, thoughts, and emotions. We need to delve deep within the ocean of our being. To do this, we need to be still. Here is a simple exercise:

Choose a quiet place where you will not be disturbed, dim the lights, sit in a relaxed posture and close your eyes.

Beginning with your toes, focus your attention on them thinking of nothing else. Progressively, advance your focus and attention to the soles of your feet and after a while begin to move your attention upwards. From your feet, move your attention through every part of your body until you reach the crown of your head. Feel your energy circulating throughout your body. After a few moments, release all and let go. Clear your mind. Be still. Become aware of the energy bathing your body.

Remain completely relaxed observing, without dwelling on anything. Do not entertain any thoughts or emotions. Just observe and be still. You are awareness.

Once you are no longer aware of your body, thoughts and emotions, what remains of you?

When all is still and you are in a void, you do not disappear. You remain inviolate. The aspect of you that remains is your real self. It is who you are, a soul personality with awareness, will and mind.

In my book ***Know Yourself, Love Yourself, Express Yourself***, I discuss the three bodies that surround the soul: the physical, the astral and the spiritual. Beyond these three is our soul, our I AM. With practice we can become aware of it and allow it to express itself through our physical body, our mind and through our emotions. It expresses itself as Love, Beauty and Joy.

DOES THE SOUL NEED TO BE SAVED?

It is not the tempest, nor the earthquake, nor the fire, but the still small voice of the Spirit that carries on the glorious work of saving souls. – Robert M

Missionaries go around instilling fear in the hearts of people in an attempt to save their souls. Many books are written and pamphlets distributed with the same theme—our souls need saving.

According to Barbara Walker, author of **The Women's Encyclopedia of Myths and Secrets,** early Christianity had to decide what it was that Christ came to save us from. They had to decide between:

1. Death;
2. Sin;
3. Demons;
4. Fleshly World and its evil demiurge.

Death

No one can save us from physical death. The body will die, disintegrate and revert back to its earthly components.

Fortunately, we are not the body. We are a living soul and the soul never dies. It is immortal. So, the soul does not need saving from something it does not experience.

Sin

If sin is a transgression against the laws of God, then our understanding of sin is primitive at best and juvenile to say the least. There are no laws that God wants us to abide by. All laws are either natural or human-made. Therefore, to transgress against a law made by man cannot be a sin. To transgress against a natural law is not a sin. It simply has consequences.

If by sin we understand a rebellion against God, that too, is primitive and immature thinking. Who can rebel against God? God is not a physical entity we can rebel against. God is a loving spirit that no one can see or oppose. To believe that a mere human can do anything to God is not only presumptuous, it is infantile. God is the Source of all.

Attributing sin to humans and offering absolution is a means of control and manipulation. It is time we cast this concept off and free ourselves of its yoke. No one is a sinner. Each and every one of us is a child of God, loved beyond measure.

The soul does not sin. The physical body can commit evil deeds at the instigation of the mind and the heart. Once we die, we leave the physical behind. Therefore, there is no body to be judged. There is only an astral body to be tormented as a result of evil deeds. The soul is pure. The impact of our actions is stored in our astral and spiritual bodies. These undergo a review after death, but this is not judgment and there is no punishment, especially eternal hell and damnation. All actions have consequences. It is the consequences of our actions that we must face and compensate for.

Fleshly World and its Demiurge

The world we live in is for us to experience, to enjoy to shepherd. Earth is a wonderfully beautiful planet. What we need to avoid while living is selfishness, abuse, bullying and taking advantage of the less fortunate.

The human body is a temple. It must be cared for, appreciated and celebrated. There is nothing in the human body to be ashamed of. Every part is miraculous.

The Demiurge:

> *The demiurge (Greek demiurgos, "craftsman") is the being who created the world in Gnosticism. The Gnostics identified him with the god of the Old Testament. The Gnostic scriptures portray him as ignorant, malicious, and utterly inferior to the true God who sent Christ to earth to save humankind from the demiurge's evil world.*
>
> Gnosticism Explained

We do not have to worry about the Demiurge. All we have to do is to adopt Christ and His teachings, especially as revealed in His parables. Christ is sufficient. He has shown us the way, the truth and how to best live a life of love and service.

* * * * *

So, does the soul need saving?

Yes, but not for the above-mentioned reasons. There is a reason embedded in the teachings of Christ revealed through His parables. In particular, two parables:

1. The Parable of the Sower; and

2. The Parable of the Talents.

The Parable of the Sower:

> *And he told them many things in parables, saying:*

"A sower went out to sow. And as he sowed, some seeds fell along the path, and the birds came and devoured them. Other seeds fell on rocky ground, where they did not have much soil, and immediately they sprang up, since they had no depth of soil, but when the sun rose they were scorched. And since they had no root, they withered away. Other seeds fell among thorns, and the thorns grew up and choked them. Other seeds fell on good soil and produced grain, some a hundredfold, some sixty, some thirty. He who has ears, let him hear." Matt 13:3-9

The Parable of the Talents:

"For it will be like a man going on a journey, who called his servants and entrusted to them his property. To one he gave five talents, to another two, to another one, to each according to his ability. Then he went away. He who had received the five talents went at once and traded with them, and he made five talents more. So also he who had the two talents made two talents more. But he who had received the one talent went and dug in the ground and hid his master's money. Now after a long time the master of those servants came and settled accounts with them. And he who had received the five talents came forward, bringing five talents more, saying, 'Master, you delivered to me five talents; here I have made five talents more.' His master said to him, 'Well done, good and faithful servant. You have been faithful over a little; I will set you over much. Enter into the joy of your master.' And he also who had the two talents came forward, saying, 'Master, you delivered to me two talents; here I have made two talents more.' His master said to him, 'Well done, good and faithful servant. You have been faithful over a little; I will set you over much. Enter into the joy of your master.' He also who had received the one talent came forward, saying, 'Master, I knew you to be a hard man, reaping where you did not sow, and

gathering where you scattered no seed, so I was afraid, and I went and hid your talent in the ground. Here you have what is yours.' But his master answered him, 'You wicked and slothful servant! You knew that I reap where I have not sown and gather where I scattered no seed? Then you ought to have invested my money with the bankers, and at my coming I should have received what was my own with interest. So take the talent from him and give it to him who has the ten talents. For to everyone who has will more be given, and he will have an abundance. But from the one who has not, even what he has will be taken away. And cast the worthless servant into the outer darkness. In that place there will be weeping and gnashing of teeth.' "When the Son of Man comes in his glory, and all the angels with him, then he will sit on his glorious throne. Before him will be gathered all the nations, and he will separate people one from another as a shepherd separates the sheep from the goats. And he will place the sheep on his right, but the goats on the left. Then the King will say to those on his right, 'Come, you who are blessed by my Father, inherit the kingdom prepared for you from the foundation of the world. For I was hungry and you gave me food, I was thirsty and you gave me drink, I was a stranger and you welcomed me, I was naked and you clothed me, I was sick and you visited me, I was in prison and you came to me.' Then the righteous will answer him, saying, 'Lord, when did we see you hungry and feed you, or thirsty and give you drink? And when did we see you a stranger and welcome you, or naked and clothe you? And when did we see you sick or in prison and visit you?' And the King will answer them, 'Truly, I say to you, as you did it to one of the least of these my brothers, you did it to me.' Matt 25:14-30

The lesson of the Parable of the Sower is for us to know that the Sower is God, the Source and our souls are the seeds. Christ explained that the seeds are the words of God. **We are the work of God and within us is the word of God as our soul.**

The lesson of the Parable of the Talents is for us to remember that initially we are gifted with one seed, one talent, a simple soul. We are expected to invest this talent and multiply its value by burying it as a seed in our hearts and minds. Next, we must nurture it so it grows and blossoms.

Our hearts and minds are the soil where this seed is dropped. In other words, this seed, the one talent is the soul within us. We must use our minds and hearts to help it grow.

As explained by Christ, there are three ways we can *"lose our seed, the soul"* and only one way we can *"save our seed, the soul"*.

Three ways to lose our seed, the soul

1. Seeds falling on the path and birds devouring them.

If we ignore our soul and become completely occupied by trivia, then we have no soul growth. There are many distractions on the highways and byways of life. If we succumb to them, we lose our way. We waste our opportunity to invest in ourselves and cultivate our souls.

2. Seeds falling on rocky ground.

If we have eyes, but refuse to see; if we have ears, but refuse to hear; if we have closed minds and refuse to think; if our hearts are hard like a rock devoid of empathy, sympathy and compassion, then we have no soul growth.

3. Seeds falling between thorns and are choked.

If we are full of doubt, worry, fear, and negativity, then our seeds have no chance to grow. They are choked. We have no soul growth.

The only way to save our seed, the soul

Seeds falling on good soil and yielding an abundance.

If our minds are receptive, our hearts are compassionate and eager to nurture, then any seed falling into our fertile soil will find a loving environment and a nurturing home. The seed will establish a root system and begin to grow. Our talent will multiply and our soul will flourish and blossom. We will not only have a soul but we will also ensure our immortality.

* * * * *

Which souls are wasted and which souls are saved is up to us. We decide if our soul will be saved or wasted by the decisions we make and the actions we take.

The Bible implies that there are only 144,000 who will be saved.

> *And I heard the number of the sealed, 144,000, sealed from every tribe of the sons of Israel: Rev 7:4*

> *Then I looked, and behold, on Mount Zion stood the Lamb, and with him 144,000 who had his name and his Father's name written on their foreheads. Rev 14:1*

Looking further into this number, I soon realized that it has nothing to do with those who have souls, or the ones who are saved.

> *No one could learn that song except the 144,000 who had been redeemed from the earth. It is these who have not defiled themselves with women, for*

> they are virgins. It is these who follow the Lamb wherever he goes. These have been redeemed from mankind as firstfruits for God and the Lamb, Rev 14:3-4

As soon as I read the above passages, I knew that the number 144,000 cannot refer to those who have souls, for these 144,000 were virgins. I do not believe those who have souls have to physically be virgins, unless by virgin is meant those who are pure at heart.

Why this emphasis on virginity? How can anyone be defiled by a woman?

Early Christianity assumed that the road to sanctity was through chastity. This is true, but chastity refers to those who are pure in heart and spirit, not physical abstinence from sex. Abstinence is unnatural. It leads to repression and abnormal outlets including abuse.

I happen to believe that sex can be noble, enriching and even a means to spirituality if it is based on love. Sex plays a critical role by ensuring the survival of the species. It also brings people together and enables them to share intimacy, tenderness and love which are critical to health, well-being and spiritual growth.

Why is the Bible so set against intimacy? Why would entire cities be bombed and destroyed because its inhabitants were enjoying sex? (Sodom and Gomorrah) And why would the Lord destroy all inhabitants of Earth because they had become corrupt by engaging in sex? (The Great Flood) Sex can never be a defilement unless it is abusive. Having sex can never be a sin because the urge is instilled in us by nature.

Instead of blaming women as defilers, what we need is a system that ensures the elimination of selfishness, abuse and taking advantage of others. It is unrealistic to condemn all sex except through marriage. It is also unconscionable to blame Eve as a temptress. What Eve did was noble, courageous and commendable. Who would not want their eyes opened to see clearly and to understand? Eve is a hero and the belief in original sin is demeaning, misleading and misguided. It is time to free ourselves of this notion that not only lowers our self-esteem as beloved children of God, but also gives the clergy an opportunity to have power and control over us.

Religion condemns sinful people. Sinful people have the hope of forgiveness and redemption. We should pity those who are without a soul for they have no hope of forgiveness or redemption. They are living on borrowed time for once they die, they are no more.

PART VI

An Interesting Thought

4 Questions

Final Thoughts

How One Book Altered the Course of My Life

AN INTERESTING THOUGHT

Until one has loved an animal a part of one's soul remains unawakened. – Anatole France

Do pets have souls?

For many years people refused to accept the theory of evolution as a possibility. With much pride and an inflated ego, we fought the idea. We are special we thought. We are created by God. But, so are the beasts. Evolution is evident and easy to demonstrate for ourselves. All it takes is an open mind.

Physically, we are just as the beasts are. That is how we started, as beasts. Then something happened. We acquired a personalized soul.

How did this happen?

Out of all the beasts on the planet, humans chose a few for domestication, among them horses, cattle, cats and dogs. It is my understanding that initially, no one had an individual soul. We, along with the beasts, started with group souls.

By observing our pets, we can learn how individual souls are acquired. Any pet that is individually cared for, loved and treated as a unique individual, will acquire an individual soul over time. Once pets acquire individuality, they keep it and the cycle of reincarnation begins for them. This process is ongoing.

This should give us a pause. If love, care and attention cause individualization or a separation from group soul, then the same law must apply universally. In other words, what we can do to our pets we can do for ourselves and for each other.

Care, nurturing and love cause the soul to establish a foothold and grow. While animals start as group soul, humans are a step ahead. We start with a seed, a "talent", a tiny spark of a soul. Like any seed or spark, unless they are tended to, they will die

Unlike beasts, humans have free will and freedom of choice. Unfortunately, many function from their ego and do not exercise any true choice. Most follow their appetites and the path of least resistance.

Unless we tend to, care for and nurture our souls, they will not get implanted in the soil of our minds and hearts, establish a root system and grow. Unless we grow our souls, we will not survive death.

If loving, caring and nurturing is how our pets acquire a soul, then perhaps that is how we acquired our soul initially. Someone must have cared for us, shown us love and affection to cause our individualization and the acquisition of a soul. Perhaps this is how we maintain, grow and blossom the soul. Compassion, sympathy, empathy, caring, loving and serving is the way.

We have a choice, a decision to make. Will we allocate a small portion of our time and resources to care for our souls? If, yes, then we begin by cultivating and nurturing our minds and souls with worthwhile publications and activities.

My books are specifically written with this in mind. Please consider reading and studying them, one small segment at a time. Investing in yourself is the most valuable of all investments.

Once we acquire the necessary knowledge, our eyes will open, our hearts will soften and we will see clearly and make better choices. It all starts by cultivating our minds.

Please accept the invitation that follows and take the first critical step in cultivating your mind, heart and soul.

4 QUESTIONS

Thinking individuals throughout history attempted to find answers to some of humanity's most perplexing questions. I have 4 questions that are personally meaningful to me that I want answered to my satisfaction:

1. Do I have a soul?

2. Why does evil exist?

3. Is there a purpose to life?

4. Why do we experience pain, suffer, face challenges and encounter obstacles?

My need to find a satisfying answer to the first question was overwhelming. I followed Christ's advice to *ask*, *knock* and *seek*. My questioning was passionate and persistent. I even wrote an article about it titled: **Soul, Fact or Fiction**, to no avail. I did not want to merely believe that I had a soul. I wanted to *know*. After lengthy research, reading and contemplating, I was still nowhere near finding a satisfying answer. I needed proof. Then it happened and I had my answer. I had a near-death experience. (Described in my first book, **<u>A Passion for Living</u>**, *a path top meaning* *and joy*.) From this experience. I knew that I did not have a soul, I was my soul.

The answer to the second question came to me while I was writing my 6th book, ***A Life Altering Discovery, not everyone has a soul***. I concluded that evil people do not have a soul. They are mere props in the theater of life providing those of us with souls an opportunity to confront, abate or transmute the evil. It is our responsibility to stand up to evil and put an end to it. The fire of evil must be extinguished. Living on this incredibly beautiful plant, Earth, is not rent free. It is our obligation and duty to confront evil. We cannot and should never remain silent in the face of atrocities. Evil will exist as long as we remain silent about it. It is dark energy. Darkness disappears the moment light shines. You and I are the light that must shine brightly to dispel the darkness that is evil.

The answer to the third question is summed up in a chapter in this book with the title: "The Purpose of Life."

We experience pain, suffer, face challenges and encounter obstacles because these are how we grow, learn and mature. We can avoid pain and suffering, but we will never be able to avoid facing challenges and confronting obstacles. These are the vitamins of life. They are necessities, not luxuries. We need them. They are our spiritual *"**bread**"* that will nourish and nurture our souls. Without facing challenges and overcoming them, we do not develop an epi-soul, the individual aspect of our soul that renders us as individuals.

Many acquiesce to be spoon-fed the answers to the most important questions of life. They choose the path of ***belief***. This is the easy way out, the path of least resistance. I choose the path of ***knowledge***. I want to know.

One of the biggest tragedies of life is that humans, the only beings endowed with freedom of choice, choose not to use it. Most abdicate their personal responsibility to find out for themselves. Our freedom of choice is an aspect of our soul, the one *"**talent**"* we are endowed with. We are expected to at least double this *"**talent**"* in our lifetime, else we will lose that which we now have. Use it, or lose it, is a law of life. I choose to use my freedom of choice to cultivate my mind and to nurture my epi-soul. I hope you will do the same. That is why I learn, teach and publish books. It is my mission and the purpose of my life.

FINAL THOUGHTS

I love planet Earth. It is such a beautifully diverse wonder to behold. We are not meant to subjugate it or its inhabitants and have dominion over all. We are here as custodians, as guardians. Our responsibility, if we choose to accept it, is to transform it into a garden and an orchard where all of its inhabitants coexist harmoniously.

We cannot exist on the planet on our own. We need the bees and the other pollinators to do their job. We owe them our existence.

We need the immense biome in our guts to do their part. Without the bacteria, the fungi and the viruses symbiotically coexisting within us, we will not survive. In fact, there are more of them in us than our own cells.

What if we did not have fruit trees and vegetables, cows, chickens, horses, pigs and fish? Would we be able to survive?

Our planet is beautiful and worthy of being tended to. Yet some people are not aware of the damage they are inflicting on the planet and on each other.

It saddens me that our planet is continuously at war. I do not recall a time in my lifetime or in our history where there were no wars.

Here we are, in the 21st century and we still resort to war to solve our conflicts. Why are we so barbaric? There is no other way to say it; **<u>war is barbaric and those who engage in it are barbaric.</u>**

It is hard to understand human nature. How can we, in good conscience, bomb hospitals, schools and ambulances?

How can we continue to murder innocent people as collateral damage of war?

How can we endure so much violence, hatred and criminality and for so long?

Savagery, brutality and inhumanity have been with us for far too long.

Christ experienced it. He had to deal with the same type of people. He referred to them as those "who have eyes, but cannot see. They have ears, but they cannot hear. They have hearts hard like a rock, so they cannot feel." (paraphrased).

Recently, while following the news of yet more atrocities in the Middle East, suddenly, it dawned on me. Perhaps these people do not have souls!

Anyone who knowingly and willingly inflicts pain and suffering on others is without a soul.

Anyone who kills and murders others who have not done any harm to them are without a soul.

Any nation that knowingly bombs hospitals, schools or the gathering places of innocent people is without a soul.

Anyone, whether a nation or individuals, who bully others because they can, are without a soul.

Anyone, whether a nation or individuals, who believe they are superior, privileged or chosen and are above all others are without a soul.

Anyone without love in their heart, blind to beauty and incapable of experiencing joy is without a soul.

Anyone who steals from the less fortunate to enrich themselves cannot have a soul.

Anyone without compassion, empathy and sympathy is

without a soul.

Anyone who cannot forgive has no soul.

Anyone who is selfish and is unable to feel how others feel cannot have soul.

Anyone who is blind to the needs of others, looks the other way and does not lend a helping hand is without a soul.

Anyone who cannot serve others gladly, selflessly and freely is without a soul.

Those whose egos are so inflated are like balloons. Once they die, the balloon will burst, the "hot air" will escape and there will be nothing left of them, for the ego dies when the body dies.

Isn't it ironic that those with the biggest egos are the ones who fall the hardest? When we die, so does the ego and if that is all we are, then once we die, we are obliterated.

Those who have poles in their eyes and yet manage to see and criticize the speck in someone else's eye are not only hypocrites, but they are also the modern day "Pharisees."

In the Parable of the Talents, Christ makes it clear, not only what we are expected to do, but also our fate if we choose not to do it.

We start life with one "talent." This is our original soul, a gift from God, the spark of divinity within us. We are expected to invest this talent, nurture it and grow it, and at least double its original value by the end of our lifetime.

If we bury it, or in other words, we do not use it and allow it to grow, then it will be taken from us and we will end up with nothing. We will be without a soul and when we die, that will be our end. Dust to dust and nothing else will remain of us.

Soul is Love, Beauty and Joy with the attributes of mind

and consciousness. By mind, I do not mean the brain and its functions which we share with the beasts. I allude to the higher faculties of mind such as creativity, imagination, visualization, contemplation, critical thinking, openness to inspiration and the ability to listen to the Voice Within.

If we do not raise our consciousness above that of the beasts, then we are not using our talents and gifts and our soul will not grow.

Living on Earth is not rent free. We have been gifted aplenty. We have a responsibility to reciprocate by being appreciative, thankful and grateful to the gift giver. We do this by exercising our freedom of choice and by devoting a portion of our time and resources to cultivate our souls.

This is the rent we must pay. If we do not, we will be evicted. We will lose that little bit of soul that we have and end up with nothing.

Right now we might have a soul. Will we have it once we die? Not if we remain barbaric, heartless, soulless and insensitive to the plight of the weak and the misery of the less fortunate.

It is not enough to not participate in barbarism. We must do what we can to end it.

It starts by rejecting violence wherever we find it starting with the gods we worship. We should never worship violent gods or fear them either. We should completely ignore them and focus instead on the God of Love, Beauty and Joy.

Not examining our beliefs is the same as acquiescing to what is perpetrated in the name of religion and those monstrous deities.

We are human. Within us is a spark of divinity. It is in the form of absolute Love, total Beauty and unsurpassed Joy. It is useless to have it and not express it. Let us shine our light brightly from the mountaintop and dispel darkness!

Ye are the light of the world. A city that is set on

an hill cannot be hid. Neither do men light a candle, and put it under a bushel, but on a candlestick; and it giveth light unto all that are in the house. Let your light so shine before men, that they may see your good works, and glorify your Father which is in heaven. Matt 5:14-16

HOW ONE BOOK ALTERED THE COURSE OF MY LIFE

Soon after I was stationed at Ft. Meade, Md, I befriended a man from Chicago, IL. His name was J. T. One day, out of the blue, J. T offered me a book as a gift. This book was: **_The Greatest Salesman in the World_** by **Og Mandino**. This one book altered the course of my life for the better. I would like to acquaint you with seven books, any of which can do the same for you and for anyone else you care about.

I have labored long and hard to find answers to the perplexing questions of life. My persistence to know inspired me to find answers that satisfy. I made many discoveries, and in the process, seven life altering books were born.

Our lives are short. Our time is valuable. We are gifted with free will. We can choose what we do with our time and our lives. It behooves us to use some of it to cultivate our minds and nurture our souls. These are the treasures that do not spoil.

The greatest gifts we have been given are talents, skills and abilities. These are obvious. What is less obvious are the gifts of time and free will. Unless we make the right choices in life, we do not advance. How or if we use our talents, skills and abilities is a choice; so is developing additional talents, skills and abilities. The quality of our life rests in our hands based on the choices we make and the actions we take.

The easiest way to advance our station in life is to increase our knowledge, but knowledge is not information. The most valuable knowledge is that which stems from experience, ours or someone else's. All of my books are based on experiential knowledge and inspiration. A little investment on your part using what I learned will yield a large return. What do I gain from making this offer?

I live to make a difference in our world. I love our incredibly beautiful planet. I want to see peace, prosperity and joint ventures the world over. My mission is to be a light that dispels darkness in all of its forms: ignorance, rigidity of heart and mind, and intolerance. I want us to have eyes that see, ears that hear and hearts that feel. By writing, teaching and by making these books available to you, I achieve my purpose.

We deserve better and it is up to us. Together, you and I can make a difference. We are all children of a loving God and we are here to do our part. We have a job ahead of us. We must accept our role and do our part.

If I, born in Syria to almost illiterate parents, in a repressive environment whose language isn't even English, am willing to do my part, so can you. We are not powerless.

The more we use what we already have, the more will come our way. That is what I discovered, learned and applied in my life. If we wisely do what we now can do, more doors will open up for us. That is a promise and it is a spiritual law.

Learn, teach, serve and be an example. Let your light shine. Do not allow others to dim your light by covering it up through disempowering beliefs, fears or threats of eternal punishment. A loving God never, ever punishes His children. God only loves.

I urge you to invest in yourself. You are valuable and your contribution is needed. It is essential that we each do our part. Consider acquiring these seven books. They will not only enrich your life, but also the lives of anyone else who might happen to read them because of you.

Seven Books to Set a New Course in Life

By Shahan Shammas. Available at Amazon.com

1. A Life Altering Discovery, not everyone has a soul

What if not everyone has a soul?

What if, of those who now have a soul, not everyone will be able to keep their soul once they die? Would you like to know how to keep yours? This book will show you, not only how to keep your soul, but also how to progressively attain conscious immortality.

Not everyone will be able to keep their soul once they die because there are more ways to lose our soul and only one way to retain it. Our soul is the one talent Christ spoke of. It is the seed dropped within us at birth as a word of God.

> Will this seed fall by the wayside where birds will devour it?
> Will it fall on hard rock where it will be scorched by heat?
> Will it fall among thorns where it will choke and suffocate?
> Or will it fall on fertile soil, establish a root system and grow to become a magnificent tree attracting the birds of the sky?

The most critical knowledge we need to have while living is how to preserve our soul so that once we die, we do not lose it. Our soul does not need to be saved from sin, for the soul never sins. It does not need to be saved from hell, suffering or eternal damnation, for the soul can never suffer. Only the physical body with its mind and emotions can suffer.

What the soul needs to be saved from is annihilation, extinction and loss forever. This will happen, according to the Parable of the Talents, if we do not invest in ourselves and cultivate our minds and hearts. We need to nurture the seed of soul and allow it to establish a root system, grow and blossom.

We are gifted with free choice. We all possess a most valuable treasure, our soul. Will we pursue trivia and squander our chance to cultivate this treasure? Or will we polish this most valuable of gems so its brilliance, brightness and light shines from the mountaintop so everyone can see it and be guided to find their way home.

This book will give us the knowledge and the resources we need to not only preserve
our soul, but to cultivate it until we finally attain conscious immortality.

2. Secret Teachings of Christ based on the parables

The secret teachings of Christ were reserved for His disciples only. Now, for the first time, they are being revealed to you. This insightful, eye-opening book will forever change how you view Christ and His parables. The Secret Teachings of Christ is a breakthrough in revealing what Christ really wanted us to know. Not only did Christ hide His most crucial teachings in the parables, He also bestowed upon us three life-altering gifts: why we should **accept and love ourselves**, why we should know that **we are important,** and that **we can make a difference**. Knowing these will surely boost our self-esteem.

The parables appear to be simple stories that Christ told His listeners. They are encoded with hidden gems of truth that He could not reveal openly lest He be stoned and killed prematurely. The parables are a clever way to preserve His teachings for posterity. The time has come to reveal these truths openly and for all. This book reveals the secret teachings of Christ based on the parables. Some of the topics include:

> What lessons can we learn from the parable of the lamp? •What does John the Baptist symbolize? •Why can't we mix new and old garments? •Who are Beelzebub and Satan? •Where is the most fertile soil to sow spiritual seeds and who is the Sower? •What

exactly is the Kingdom of Heaven? Is it within us? How do we find and use it? Why is the Kingdom of Heaven like a seed, yeast, a treasure, a pearl and a net? How can discovering the Kingdom Within transform our lives? •Why did Christ have 12 disciples? •Why would a shepherd leave 99 of his sheep to seek the one he lost? •Why must we forgive? •How can we double the talents we are entrusted with? •Who is the Prodigal Son who returns home? •Did Christ come to die for our sins? Or did we kill Him because of our sins? •Why would Christ expect a barren fig tree to produce figs? •What "fertilizer" can we use to be productive ourselves? •Why does Christ refer to "wedding feasts" in His parables? Who are invited to these feasts? •What is the significance of the numbers Christ used in His parables? •Why 10 virgins? •Why is the parable of The Good Samaritan so important? •Who is our neighbor? •What does "midnight" refer to in the parables? •Is it possible to be rich and be saved? •Are Heaven and Hell real places? •What secrets lie hidden in The Lord's Last Supper? •What does the life of Jesus Christ tell us about our lives?

For a very long time a veil has been placed over our eyes so we cannot see clearly. Ignorance, bias, presupposition and entrenched beliefs are components of this veil. We are responsible for our lives. If the truth is important to know, then we must do the work. We must seek, ask and knock until we have a satisfactory answer. This book will give us the knowledge we need to change course for an enlightened life.

3. Know Yourself, Love Yourself and Express Yourself

If you truly know yourself, you will love yourself and if you love yourself, you will express yourself. This perceptive, empowering book will show you how.

Is there a treasure that never spoils buried deep within us? Is this treasure a "talent" that we must develop? What exactly is this "talent"? How can we find it?

Developing this "talent" is our number one priority. It is the one thing that we must seek at the expense of all else. If we gain the whole world but do not discover what this "talent" is, we have wasted our life pursuing trivia. This "talent" is a secret hidden in plain view. Unless we know where to look, we will not see it. It is in Christianity and it is the Philosopher's Stone that the Alchemists were seeking.

Our lives would be simple had we been born with a guide for living, but we are not. We do not know why we are here, what we need to do with our lives or why we contract diseases, suffer and die. Yet, we can have meaningful answers for all of our questions. This book provides answers. It also demonstrates that we are not simply a physical body; we have astral and spiritual bodies as well. All three bodies must be cared for and nurtured so they can grow and blossom.

This book explains the purpose of life, provides a guide for intentional living and reveals many secrets such as the secret of Christianity, the secret of the Alchemists, the secrets of sleep and dreams, the secret of prayer, the secret of the mustard seed, the secret of the breath and the secret of the Millennium. Knowing these secrets will open our eyes and our hearts. We will know who we are and what we need to do with our lives. Our journey begins when we know ourselves intimately, love ourselves unconditionally and express ourselves fearlessly.

Some of the topics include:

>A Manual for Living •Does Life have a Purpose? •Why Are We Born, Live and Die? •We Are in a Theater •We

Are on a Journey •We Are a Work in Progress •We Are Connected •The Nature of Our Earthly Experiences •We Are a Trinity •I AM •Knowing Our Source •The Three Names of God •How Can We Know for Certain? •Concepts of Self •Accept Yourself •Forgive Yourself •Love Yourself •Love Others •The Nature of Love •The Quest for Happiness •Be Prepared, Always •Be Fearless •Highlight Your Uniqueness •Sharpen Your Toolset •Express Yourself •Secret of Christianity •Secret of the Mustard Seed •Secret of Prayer •Secret of Sleep and Dreams •Secret of the Breath •Secret of the Alchemists •Secret of the Millennium

4. Mystery Solved! human immortality revealed

What if suddenly we understood the mysteries of life and death? Why were we born? Why do we age and die? Why do we experience pain and suffering? Why does evil exist? What if we knew that our birth was not an accident? That there is a plan for our lives and this plan is of our own choosing? What if we knew why we are attracted to specific individuals, places and situations, but not by others? What if we discovered that we have a soul and that it is of the nature of God? What if we had a better understanding of what this nature is? Would any of this make a difference? How would having answers impact our lives?

This book is based on personal experience and has the power to transform our lives for the better. The revelation I received can be yours. Peace, serenity and understanding await you.

Some of the topics include:

The Human Experience •Touching Heaven •The Spark •Reflection •Dream, The Assembly •Clues About the Nature of My Self •The Miraculous •Revelation •Disadvantages of Same Body Physical Immortality •Advantages of Cyclic Immortality •Elegance of Cyclic Immortality •What Constitutes Proof? •The Evidence •Soul, Fact or Fiction •What is Soul? •Evidence in Support of Soul •Why Do Cells Divide •Birth, Where Do We Come From? •Why Don't We Remember? •Death, Where Do We Go After We Die? •Does Life Have a Purpose? •Why Attraction? •Why Do We Experience Misery, Pain and Suffering? •Where Does Our Sense of Wonder Come From? •Why Do We Dream? •The Mystery of Identity •Understanding the Nature of Life •Making the Most of This Life •Planning for Our Next Life

The Human Experience is *unique.* Make the most of it by unravelling its mysteries. The greatest gift we have is freedom of choice. We can choose to live governed by random forces where we deal with whatever happens, or we can consciously take control of our lives. We are given "talents" and placed on a stage. We are expected to invest our talents wisely. This book will help us do just that. Act and take charge. A small investment on your part will yield a great return.

5. Listening to the Voice Within, becoming enlightened

Learning to listen to the Voice Within is the shortest route to living the abundant life. This book will show us how this practice will place us on an accelerated path to finding and living our mission in life.

There is one "gift" without which we cease to be human. Plants and animals do not have it. Only humans have it. Most do not appreciate this trademark of being human or use it effectively to advance their "Happiness Quotient." In fact, many use it to their detriment. We can discover, cultivate and learn to use this gift more effectively. It requires us to be fearless, open-minded and intent on improving our lot in life. This gift is our conscience coupled with Freedom of Choice.

Listening to The Voice Within will show us how to best use our Free Will. This book will inform, empower and liberate us. It is a guide for transformation. It will help us become enlightened beings. It will push us to grow beyond our comfort zone. To grow, we must break loose of the tethers that constrict and stifle us. Life is a journey, not a destination. If we open our minds and hearts to reason and inspiration and listen to the promptings of The Voice Within, we can be transformed. We need to discover who we are spiritually, in addition to what we are materially. Our journey of awakening starts when we let go of our fears and learn to exercise our freedom of choice. We are responsible for our lives and the decisions we make. This book is full of empowering and liberating insights that have the potential to change our lives. Here are some of the topics presented in this book:

> What is the Voice Within? •Life as an Experiment •How Free Am I? •My Life as a Garden •Obey or Disobey •Am I My Brother's Keeper? •Privilege •The Transient and the Enduring •Journey to Enough •The Path Less Travelled •Energy, Force,

& Power •Human Pyramid •Natural "Enemies" of Humanity •Memory as a Photograph •Good, Bad and Evil •Transformers of the World •Perfection •Why Attraction? Why Love? •Insights I Live by •Self-Examination •Questions to Consider •Aging, Life and Death •Mystery of Dreams •Raising Our Consciousness •Soul •Who Am I? •The Word Made Flesh •As Within, So Without •In God's Image •Living in Truth •When Two or More Come Together •Good News and Sad News •Thy Kingdom Come! •The Second Coming •Brave, Enlightened World

Our journey of awakening starts when we let go of our fears and act with intelligence. The first decision we have to make is whether or not we are serious about improving the quality of our life by gaining knowledge and understanding. Once we are equipped with the right knowledge, we can act boldly. It will make a difference in how you see and interpret the events in your life.

6. The Hidden Meaning & Power of the Lord's Prayer, based on the Syriac Aramaic

The Lord's Prayer is the only specific prayer Christ asked to learn and recite. Why? This book will, not only reveal the hidden gens within the prayer, but also shares a 12-step process to effective prayer and how to make sure our prayers are heard and answered. Some of the topics include:

> ***Our Father who art in heaven.*** Who is this Father we are praying to? And where exactly is this heaven? •***Hallowed be Thy Name.*** Do we know God's name so that we may hallow it? How can we find out what this name is? •***Thy kingdom come.*** What exactly is this

kingdom and why are we asking for it to come? Is the Kingdom of God the same as the Kingdom of Heaven? •***Thy will be done on earth as it is in heaven.*** What does this mean? What is God's will in heaven that we want it done on earth as well? Is there any other will than that of God's will? •***Give us this day our daily bread.*** Why are we asking only for bread? What about some meat and potatoes as well? How about some dessert while we are at it? Does this mean we do not have to earn our livelihood? •***And lead us not into temptation.*** Who leads us into temptation? Is it God or the Devil? If it is the Devil, why are we asking God not to lead us into temptation? •***But deliver us from evil.*** What exactly is evil? And if God does deliver us from evil, does it mean that we do not face difficulties anymore? •Why did Christ teach us this specific prayer? Are there hidden gems buried within it that we need to discover?

7. A Passion for Living, a path to meaning and joy

Not much can be achieved in life without passion. Following our passion, we live a meaningful and joyous life. What can be more rewarding!

Do you know why we are here and what is the best way to live? Are we the result of an accident of nature? Were we created by God to be tested? We can have real and satisfying answers to these fundamental questions. The key is insistent desire, persistence and a demand to know. "***Ask and it will be given to you; seek and you will find; knock and the door will be opened for you.***" Matt 7:7-8. This is what Christ promised us. These are active verbs. We must take the first steps. Our asking, seeking and knocking, however, must be loud, insistent and persistent until we have our answer.

To live a life of meaning and joy, we must wake up to who we are. We must live for a purpose that embodies who we want to be. We can be victimized by our circumstances or we can choose to create the life we want. This book helps us wake up, decide on something worthwhile to live for, know ourselves, decipher the meaning of life and master the art of living. We can understand why we age and die, how to release our brakes, take it easy, do what we can and enjoy ourselves. If we apply the insights in this book, we will discover our passion for living and live a life of meaning and joy.

Some of the topics in this book include:

> Wakeful Living •We Do Not Have to Struggle to Succeed •We Have What It Takes •Have Something Worthwhile to Live For •Know Yourself •Decipher the Meaning of Life and Master the Art of Living •The Blueprint of Life and Its Architect •Understand Why We Age and Die •Eight Reasons We Decide to Die •Release Your Brakes •Ignorance, Fear, Pain and Suffering •Take it Easy, Enjoy Yourself and Do What You Can •Living Like a Corporation •Willingness to Change •Dimensions of Reality

The paperback version of **A Passion for Living, a path to meaning and joy** is available only from the author. To order it for $17.00 plus $3.95 S/H. please email your request to: shahanshammas@Gmail.com

Order 2 or more copies and the shipping is free. You can pay via PayPal, Venmo or Zelle

My name and email address are:
Shahan Shammas
shahanshammas@gmail.com

Please provide you full name, mailing address and an email in case there is a question. Once I receive your payment, I will mail you the book(s).

To face the challenges of life, we need knowledge stemming from experience. If knowledge is power, these books give us the power we need to live happy, fulfilled and meaningful lives. Instead of merely passing through life, we can wake up, live with passion and make a positive difference in our lives and the lives of others. By improving the quality of our life through knowledge, the lives of those we touch will also improve. We are each valuable because we are interconnected. If J. T. through one book altered the course of my life for the better, we can do the same.

Grab this opportunity to set your life on a new course. This is your chance. Order these books and study them. You will gain understanding and valuable insight on how to master your circumstances. With understanding comes wisdom, contentment and peace of mind. You have the power, not only to improve your life, but also to impact the lives of those you care about. Often, all it takes is a small gesture such as the gift of a valuable book.

ACKNOWLEDGEMENT

I am grateful to the Cosmic for inspiration, guidance and the required time. I appreciate the help of all those who made this book a reality especially my wife Barbara. I am indebted for her reviewing and editing. Barbara's help and support have been invaluable. Next, I would like to thank family and friends for their continued support, especially Joe Shammas for his review and suggestions.

ABOUT THE AUTHOR

Shahan Shammas

Shahan was born in Aleppo, Syria. At the age of 15, he went to Lebanon where he entered a monastery to study and prepare to be a monk. After two years in the monastery, he left to continue his education. Shahan graduated from the American University of Beirut with a Bachelor's degree in Biology. At the age of 24, Shahan left for the United States and became a US citizen while serving three years in the Army at the Medical Laboratory of Fort Meade, MD. After working as an Electron Microscopist at the Walter Reed Army Medical Center for 7 years, Shahan started a new career in Information Systems. He worked for the Treasury Department until he retired. Shahan then became a teacher at the Judy Hoyer Family Learning Center where he taught Life Skills to adults for ten years. Shahan's background is in the Sciences, Religion, Philosophy and Spirituality. Shahan has lectured extensively in the areas of acquiring knowledge, raising consciousness and actualizing the human potential.

Shahan is the author of: 1. The Secret Teaching of Christ based on the parables. 2. Know Yourself, Love Yourself, Express Yourself – an inspiring guide for intentional living. 3. Mystery Solved! Human immortality revealed. 4. Listening to the Voice Within, becoming enlightened. 5. A Passion for Living, a path to meaning and joy.

Shahan Shammas is a cultivator of the mind. He has dedicated his life to learning and teaching. His purpose is to be a light that dispels darkness, to empower those he encounters, and to be an agent for peace.

For information about Shahan's availability for speaking engagements, workshops and seminars, please email him at: shahanshammas@gmail.com

BOOKS BY THIS AUTHOR

The Secret Teachings Of Christ Based On The Parables

Know Yourself, Love Yourself, Express Yourself

Mystery Solved! Human Immortality Revealed

Listening To The Voice Within, Becoming Enlightened

A Passion For Living, A Path To Meaning And Joy

www.ingramcontent.com/pod-product-compliance
Lightning Source LLC
Chambersburg PA
CBHW071123090426
42736CB00012B/1992